This book is dedicated to parents all over the world
who are surviving and thriving in the jungles of
remote working and distance learning at home with the kids.

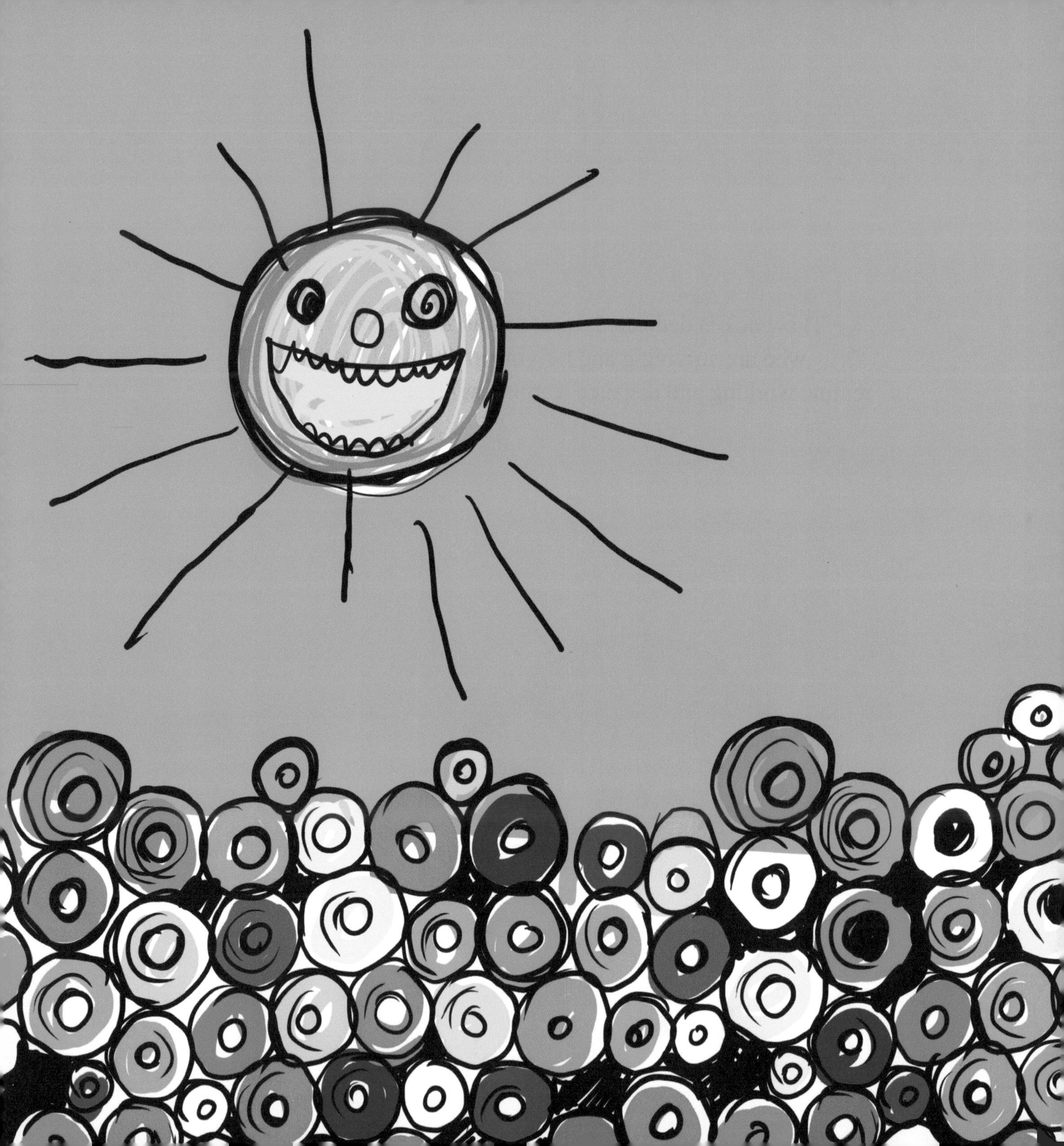

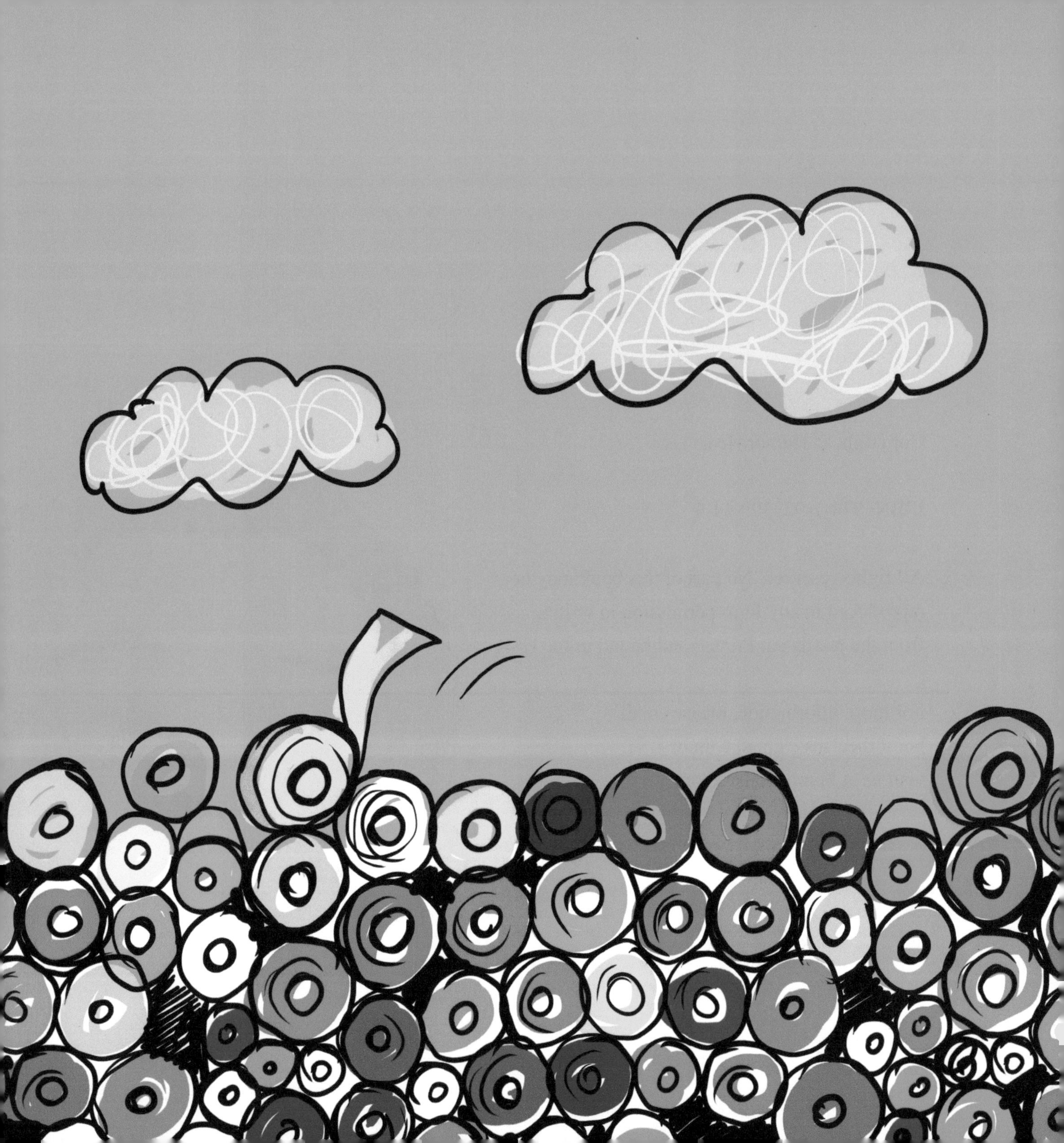

ISBN: 978-1-953399-64-9

For more information, please email humorhealsus@gmail.com or visit us at humorhealsus.com

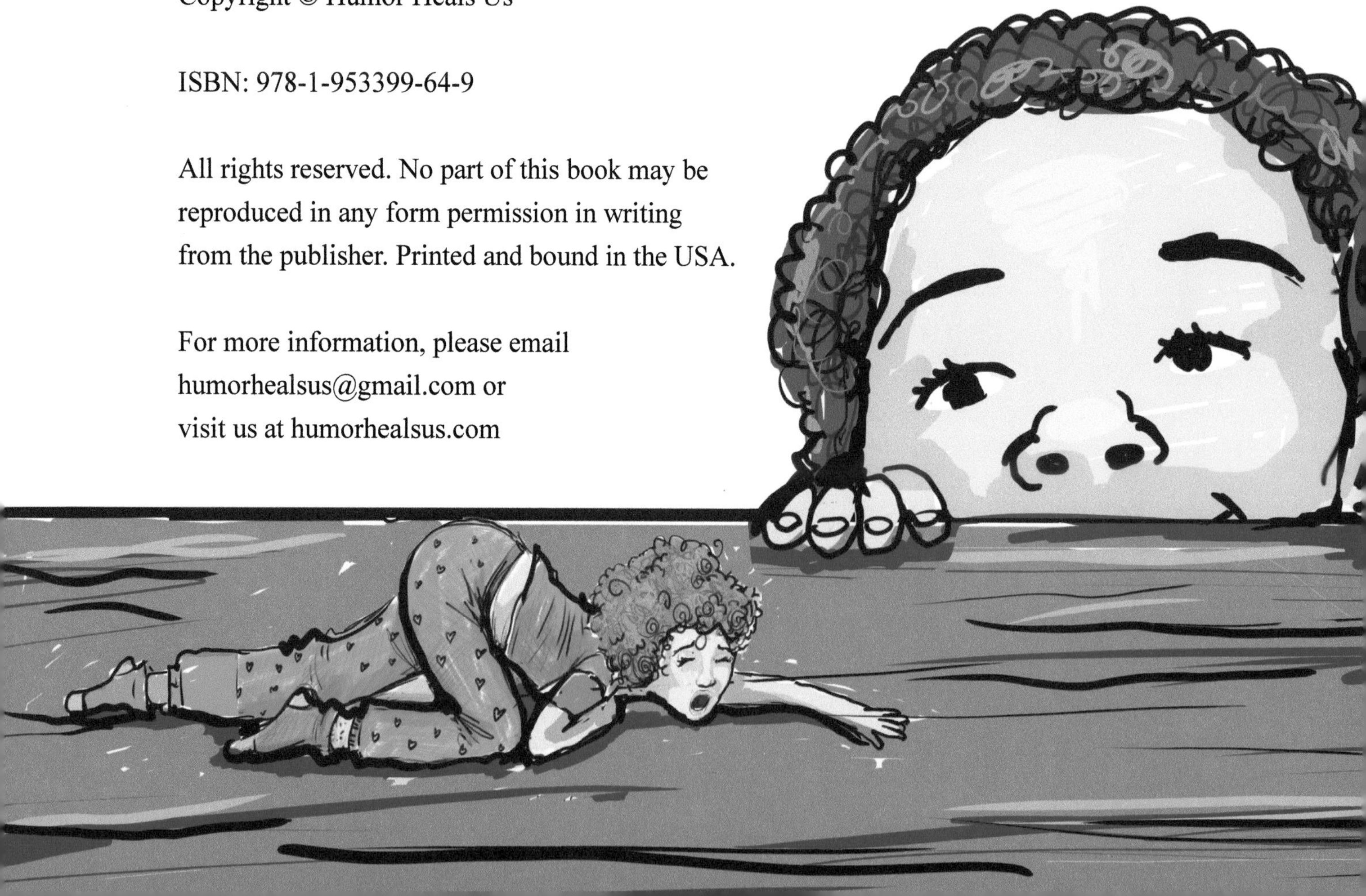

THE VERY TIRED and HUNGRY PANDEMIC MOMMY

by Humor Heals Us

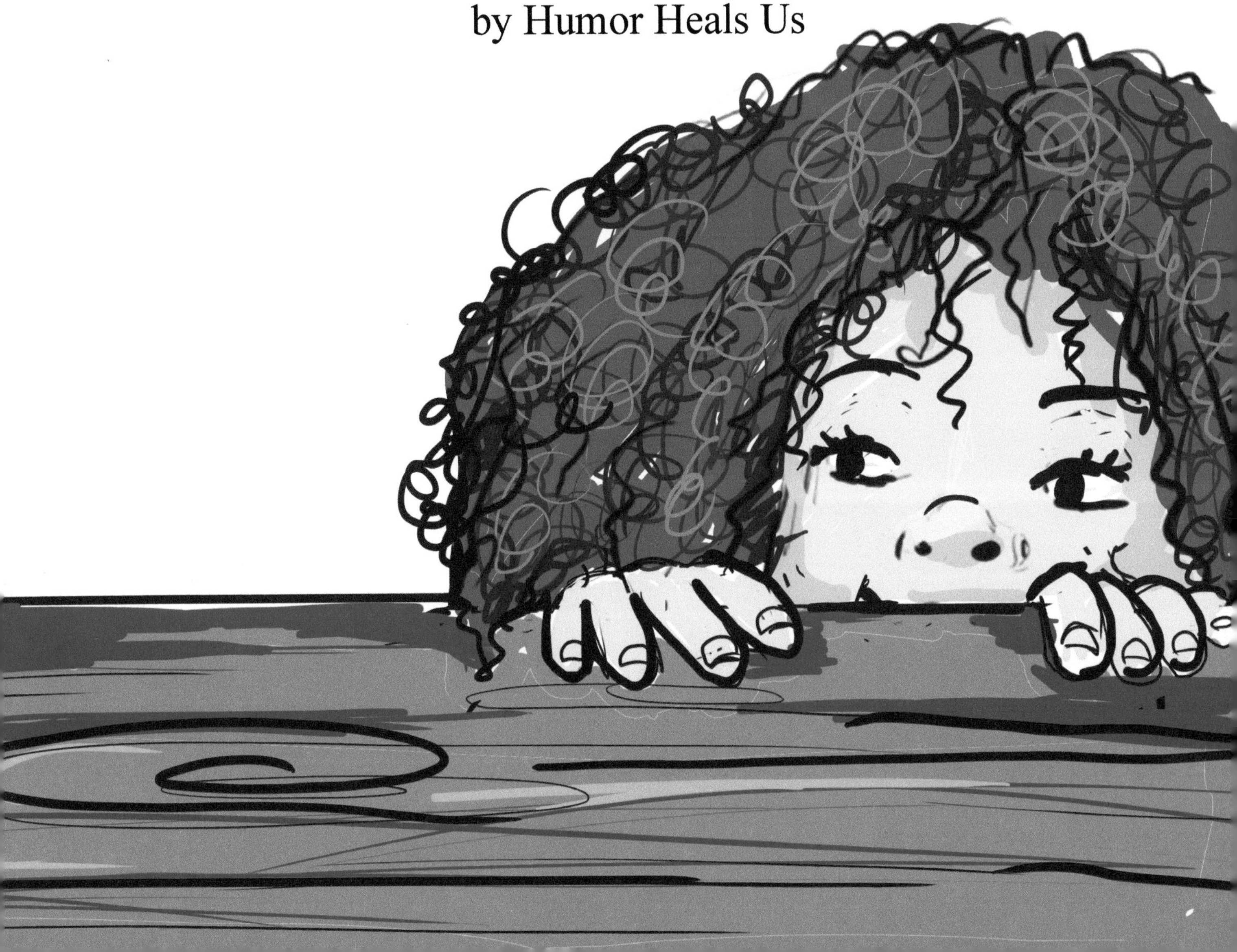

In the light of the moon

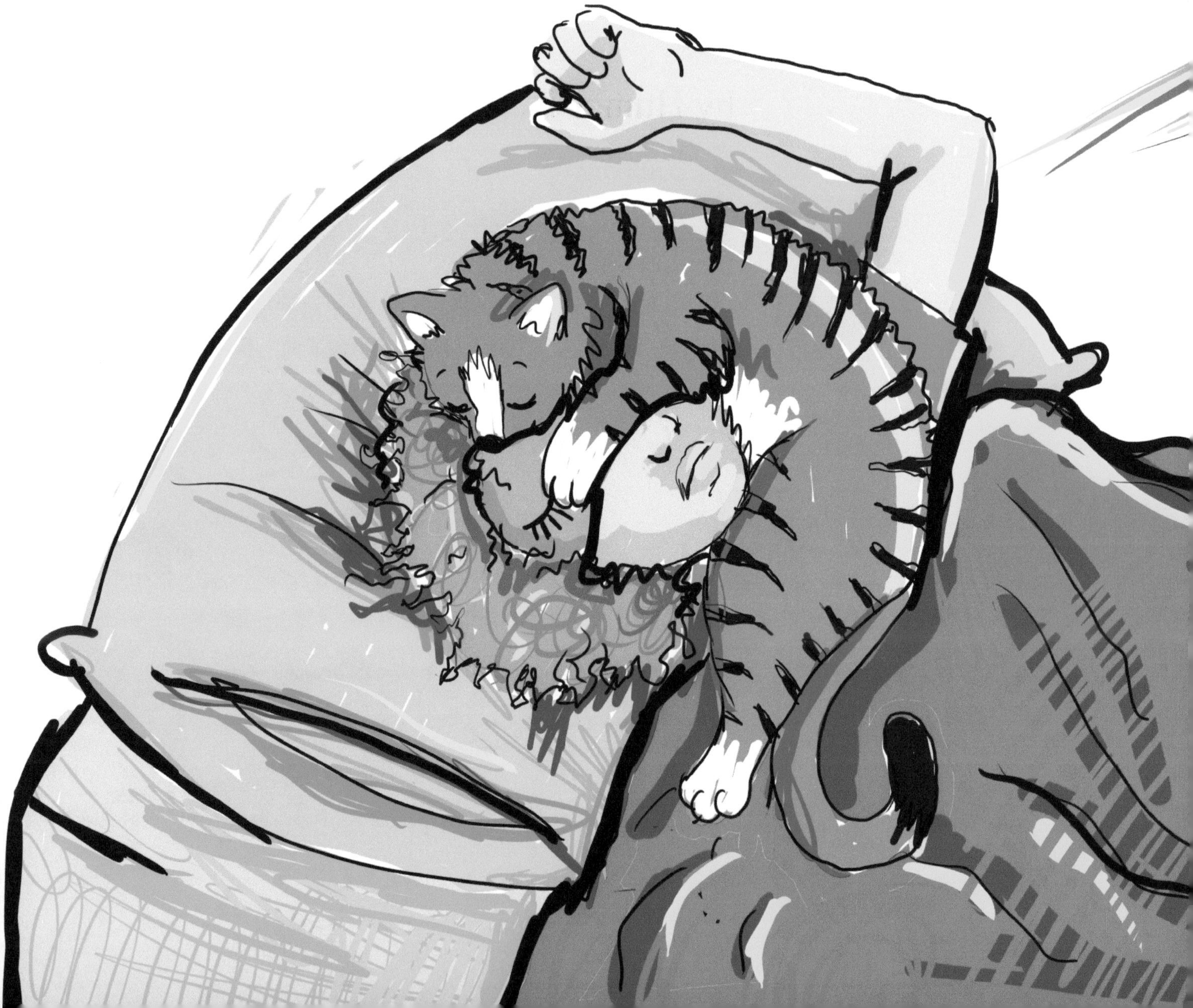

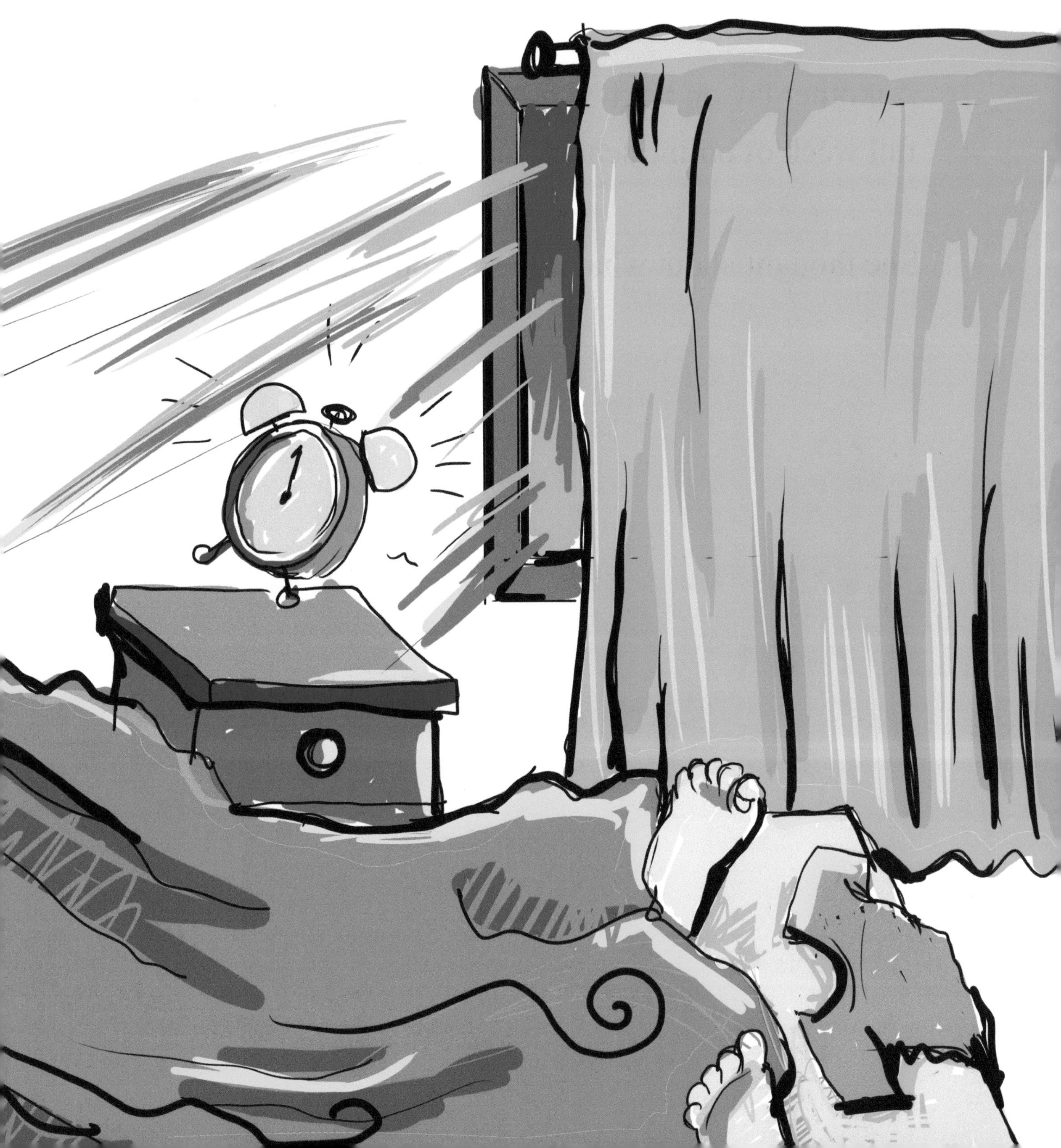

A mother lay on her bed not looking forward to another full week of online school with the kids.

She thought about what title she could give herself…

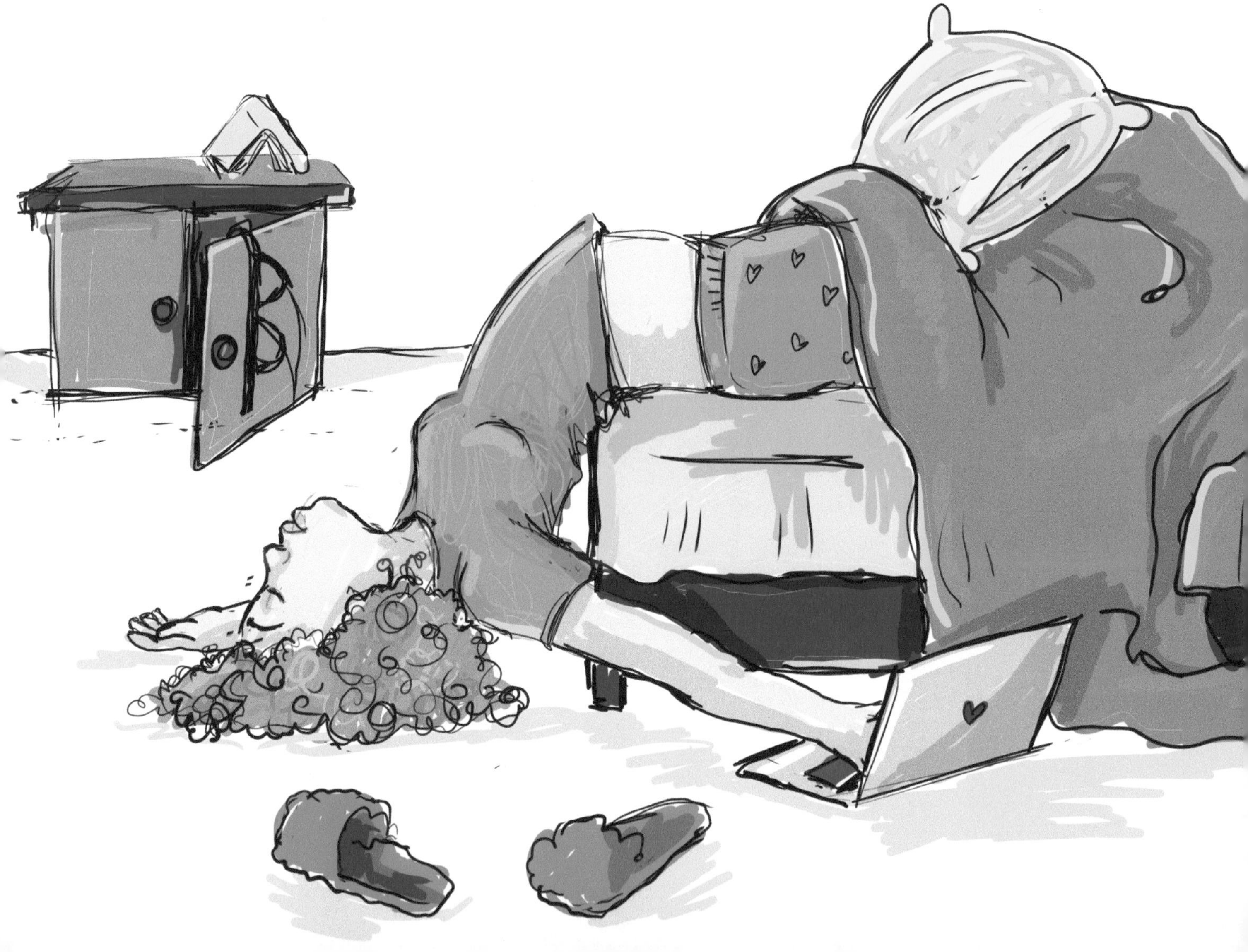

Temporary domestic educator?

Domestic engineer for Chaos Coordination?

Day Drinker?

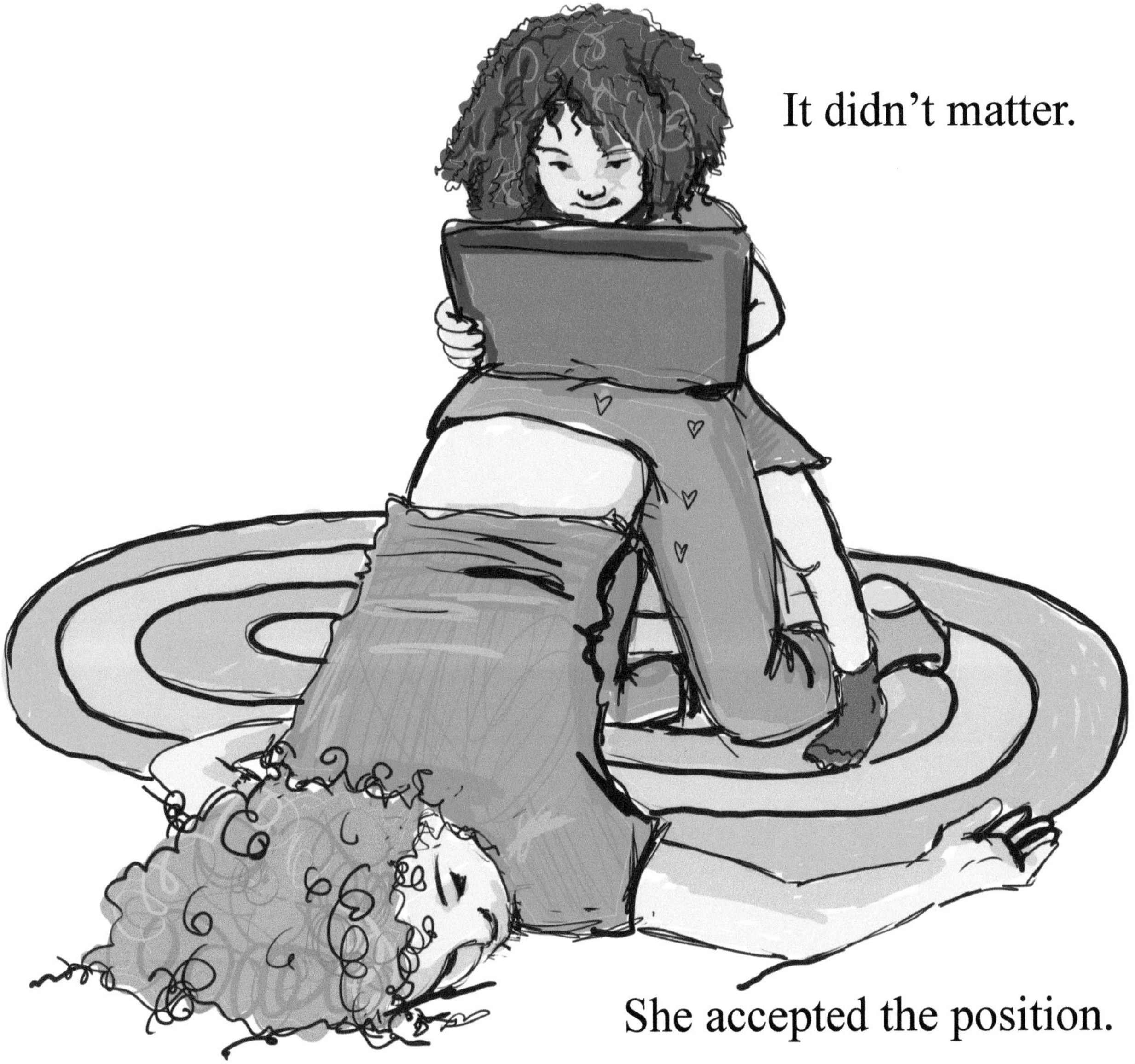

It didn't matter.

She accepted the position.

One Sunday morning the warm sun came up and... BOOM!

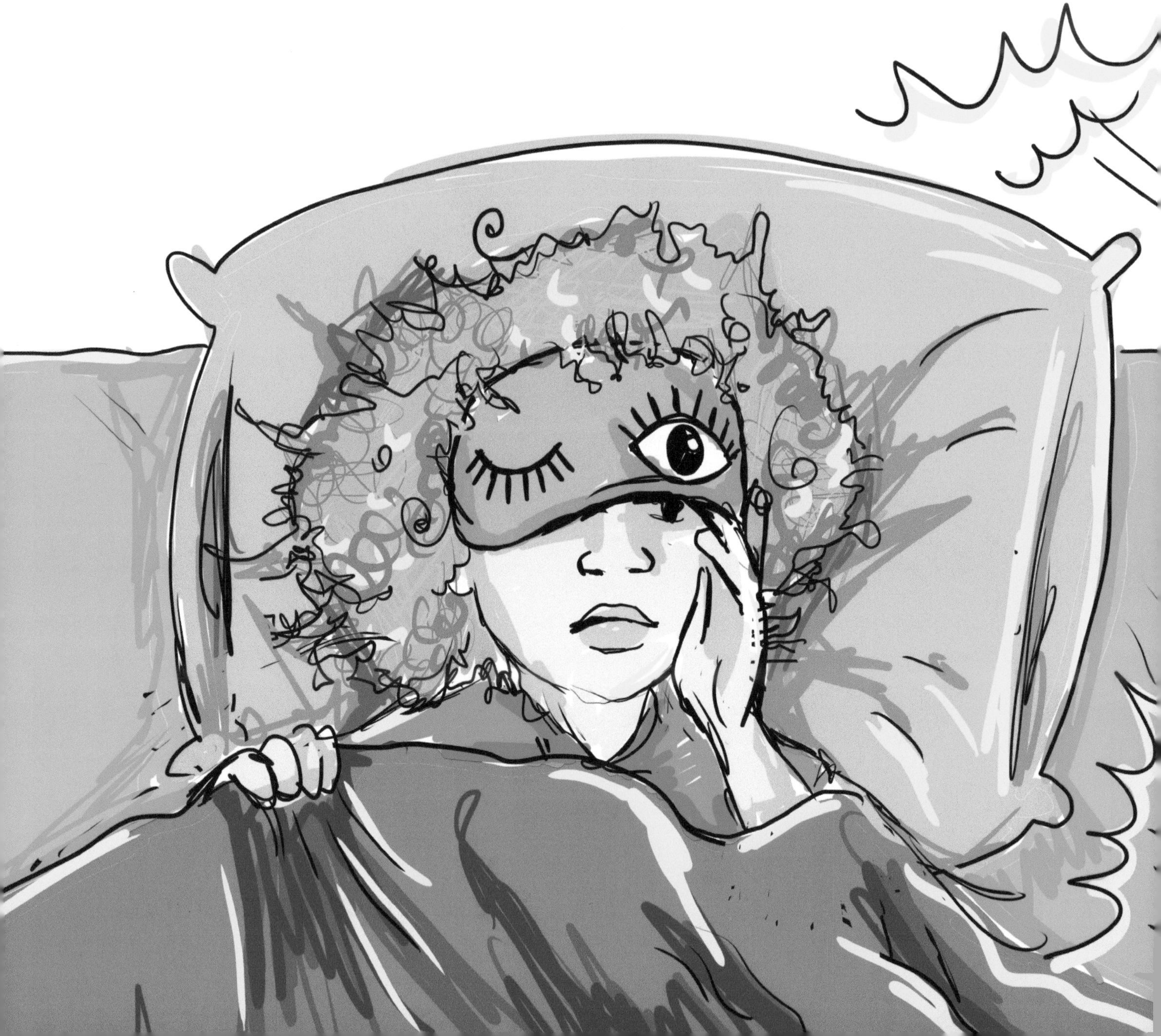

A little girl spilled her milk on the kitchen floor.

And out of the bed came a tired and hungry pandemic mommy.

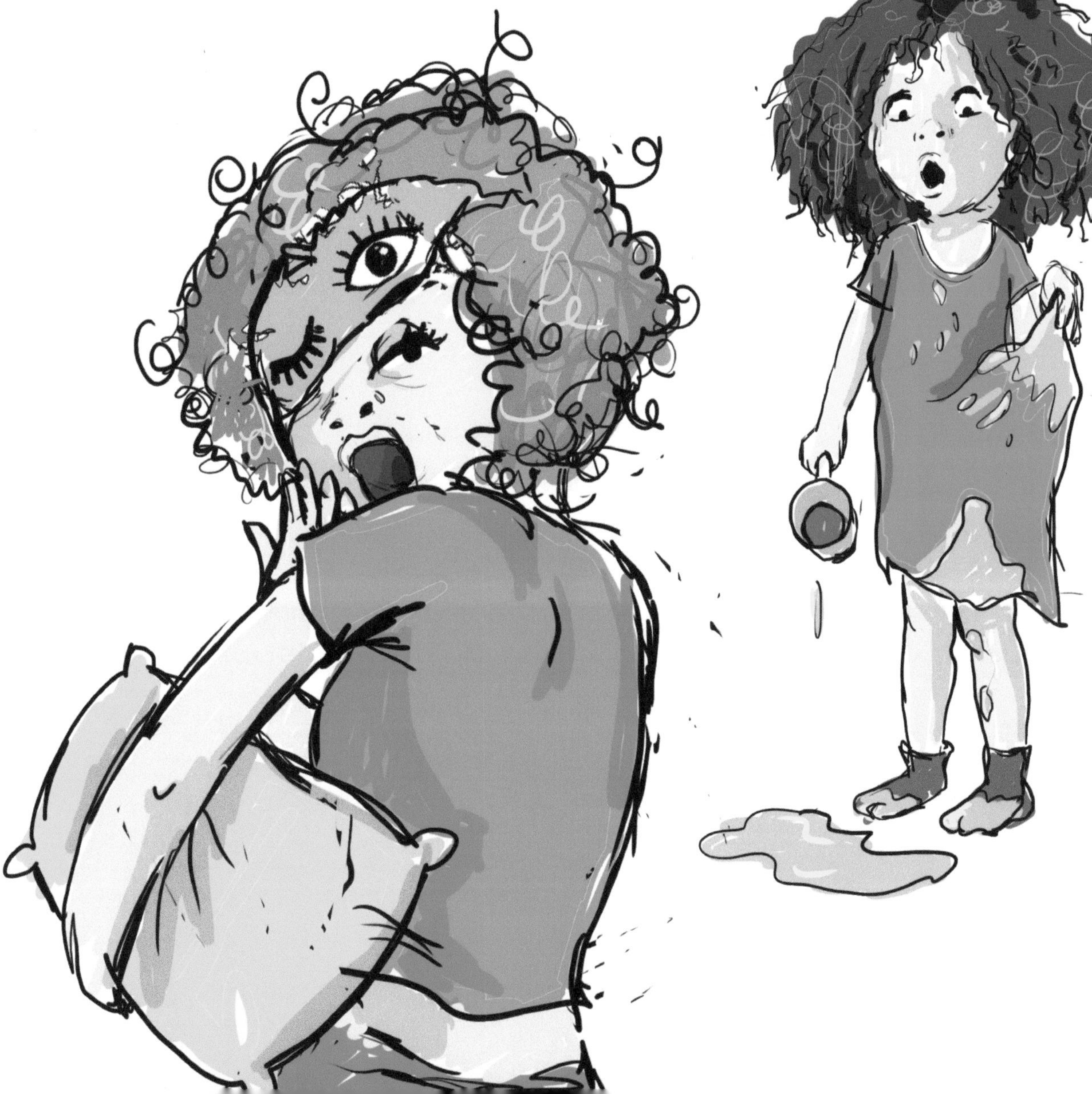

Immediately, she began to look for her coffee.

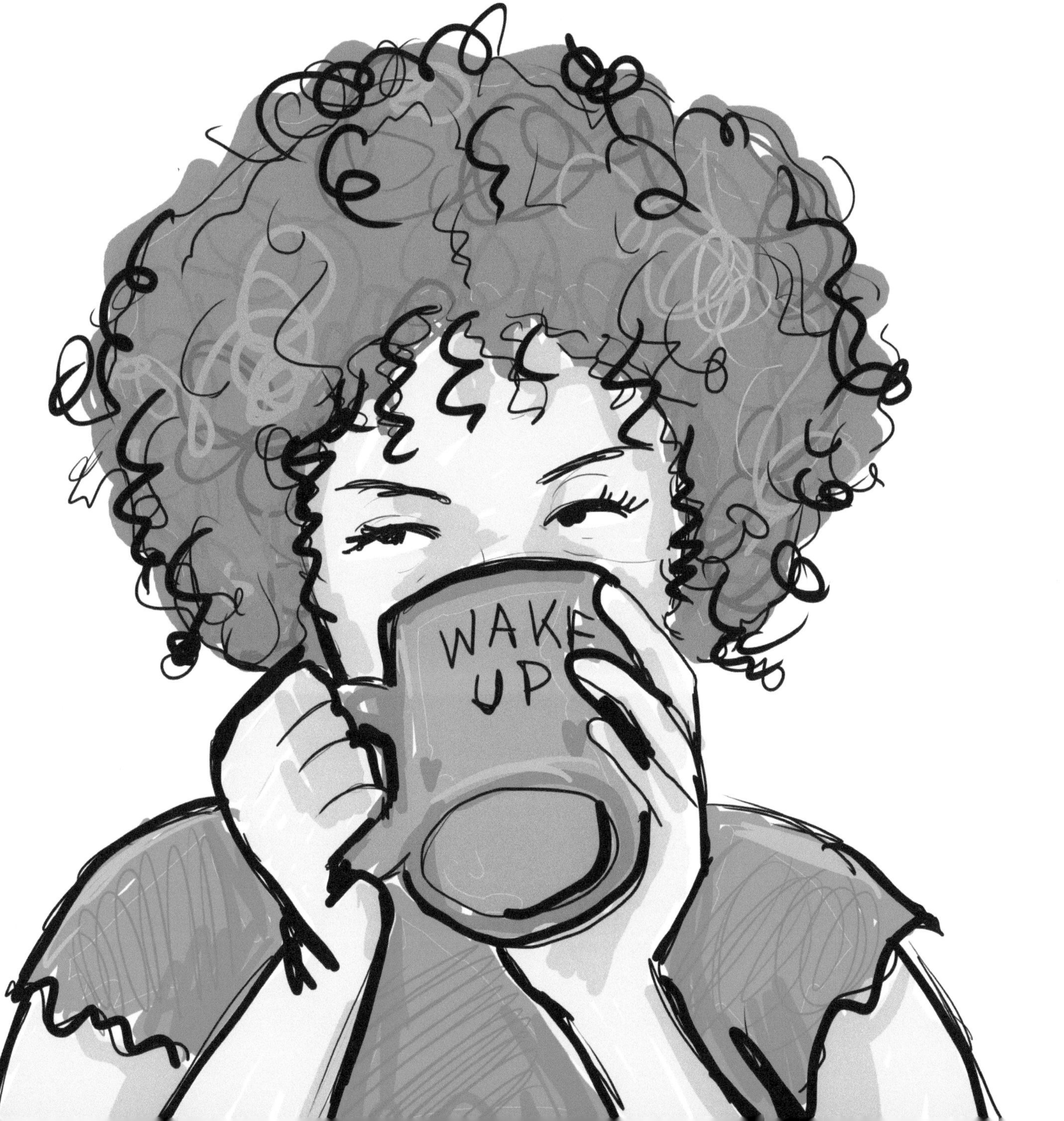
WAKE
UP

On Monday, she ate through one small cookie, while the kids met their teacher online.

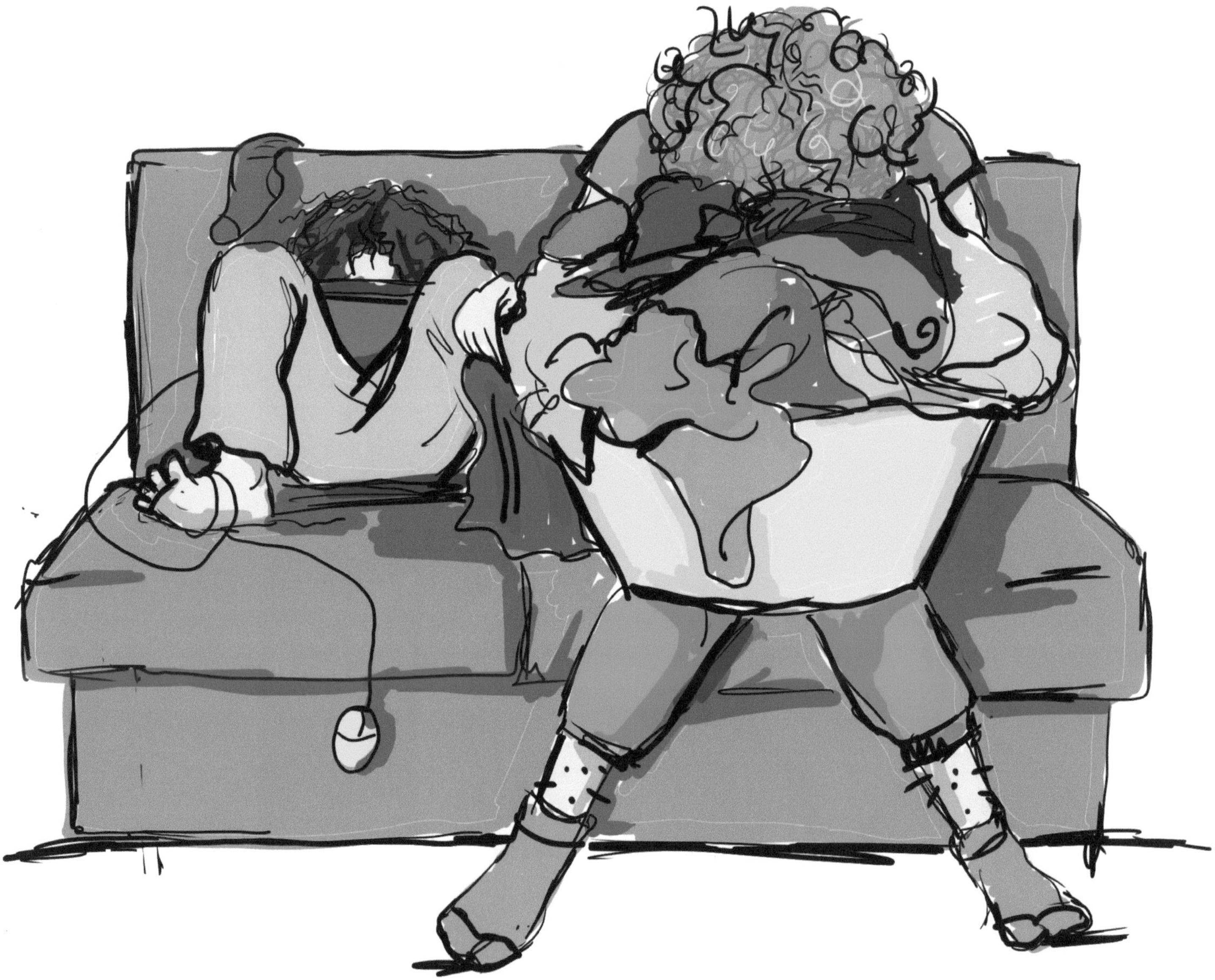

It's really not that bad, she thought to herself.

But she was still tired and hungry.

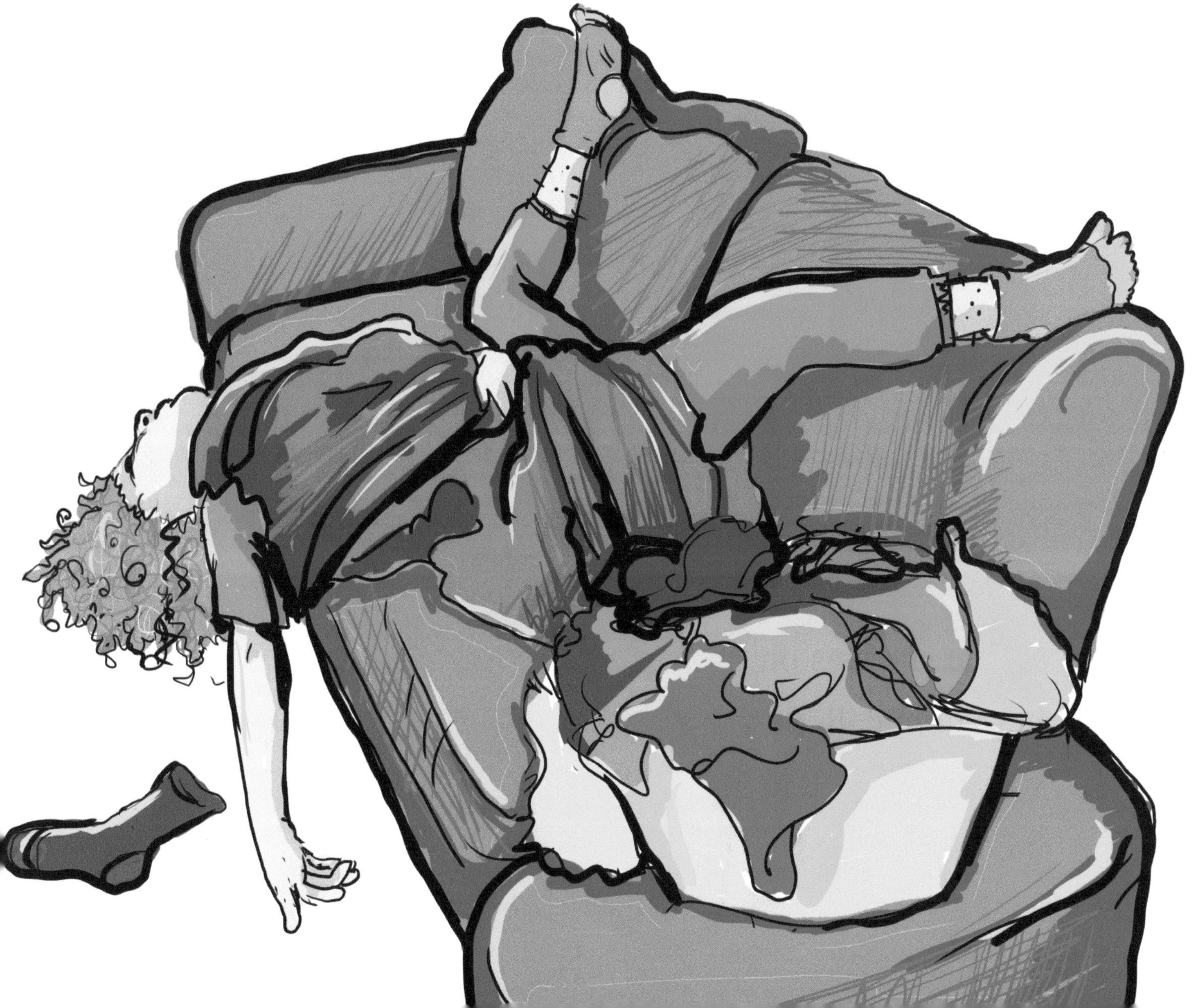

On Tuesday, she ate through two brownies when the kids lost connection to their online class.
They had forgotten to charge the device overnight.

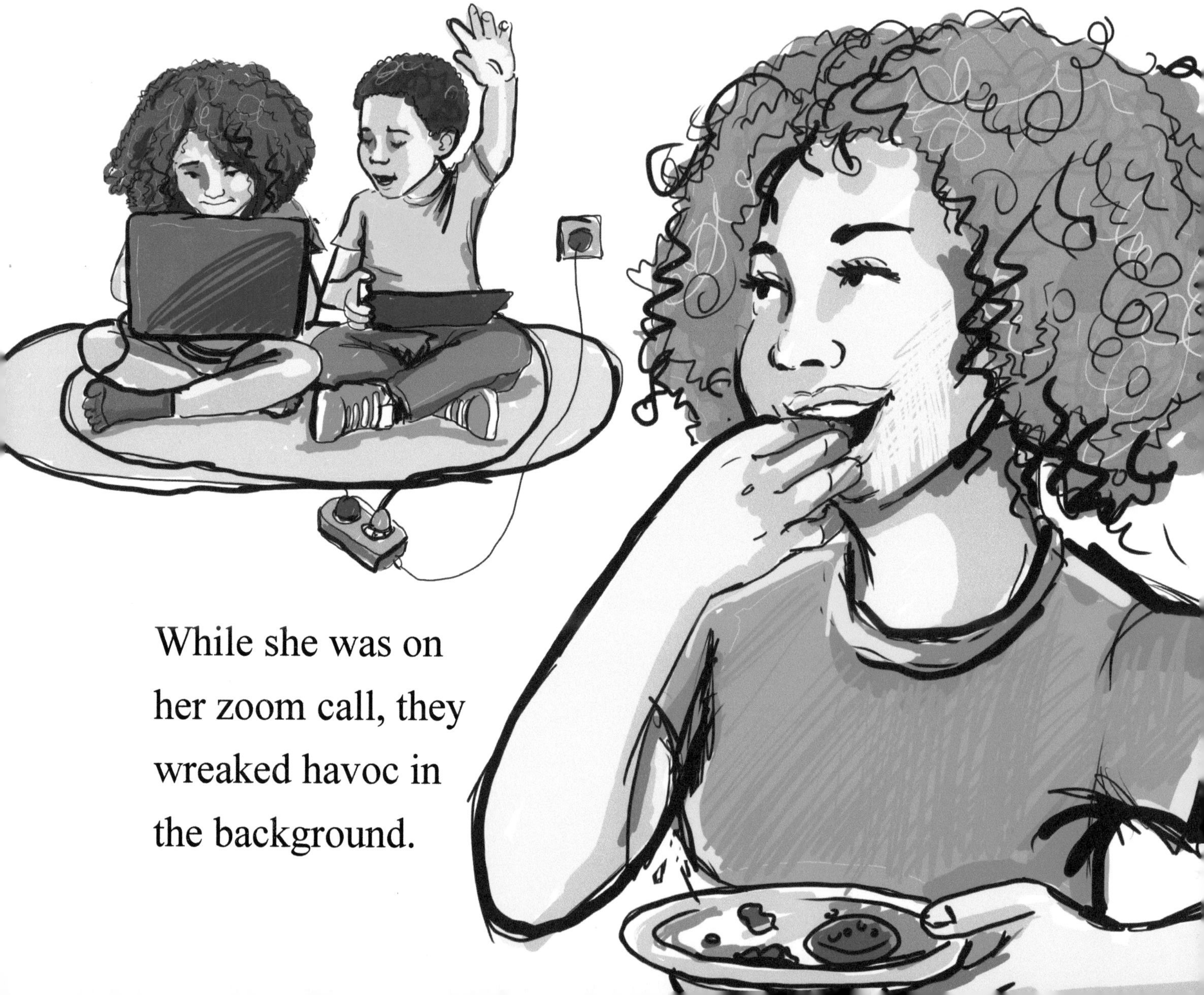

While she was on her zoom call, they wreaked havoc in the background.

Please someone send help, she thought.

But she was still tired and hungry.

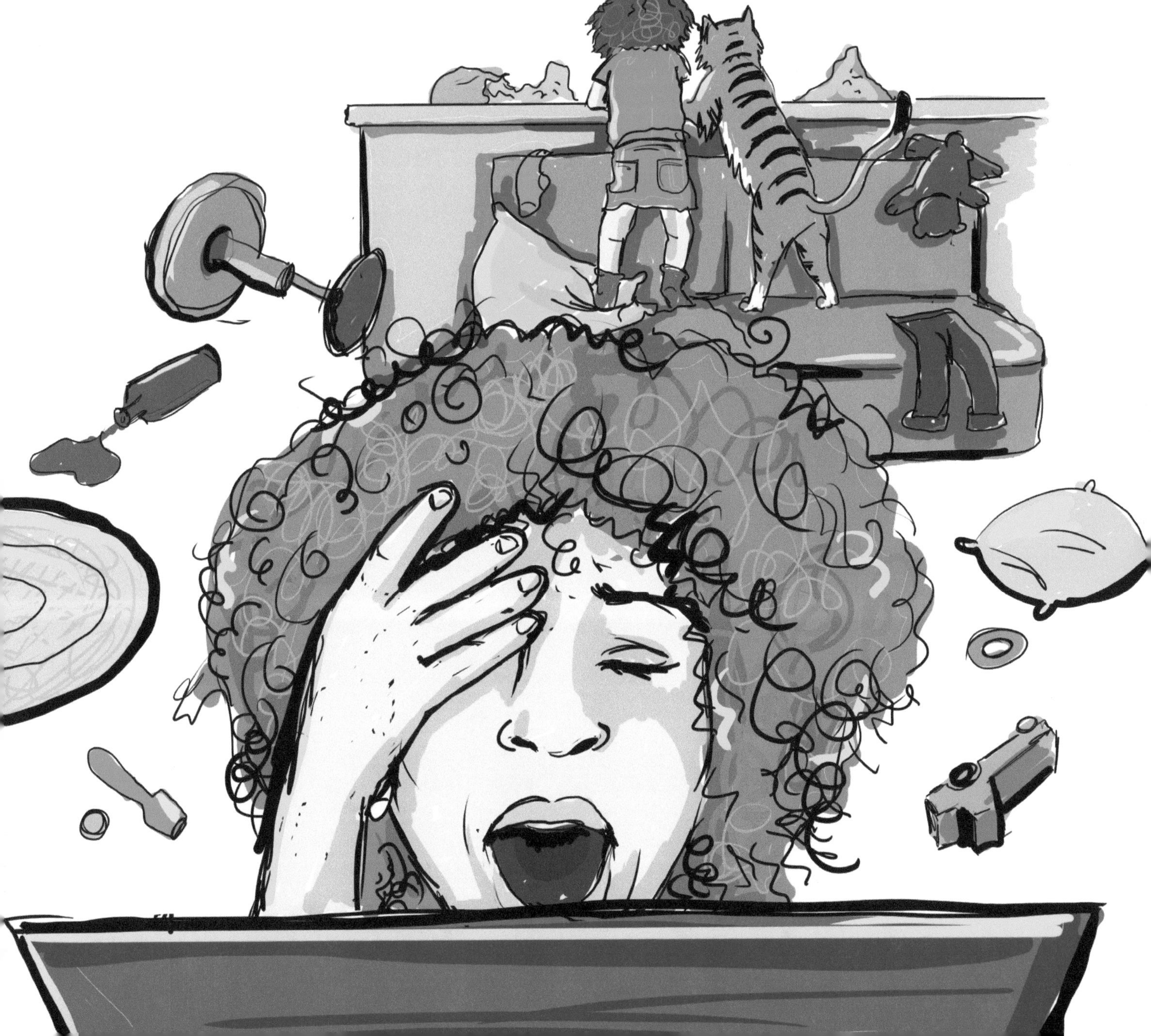

On Wednesday, as the kids declared a No Homework Day, she ate through three mini cupcakes.

She added a glass of wine for good measure.

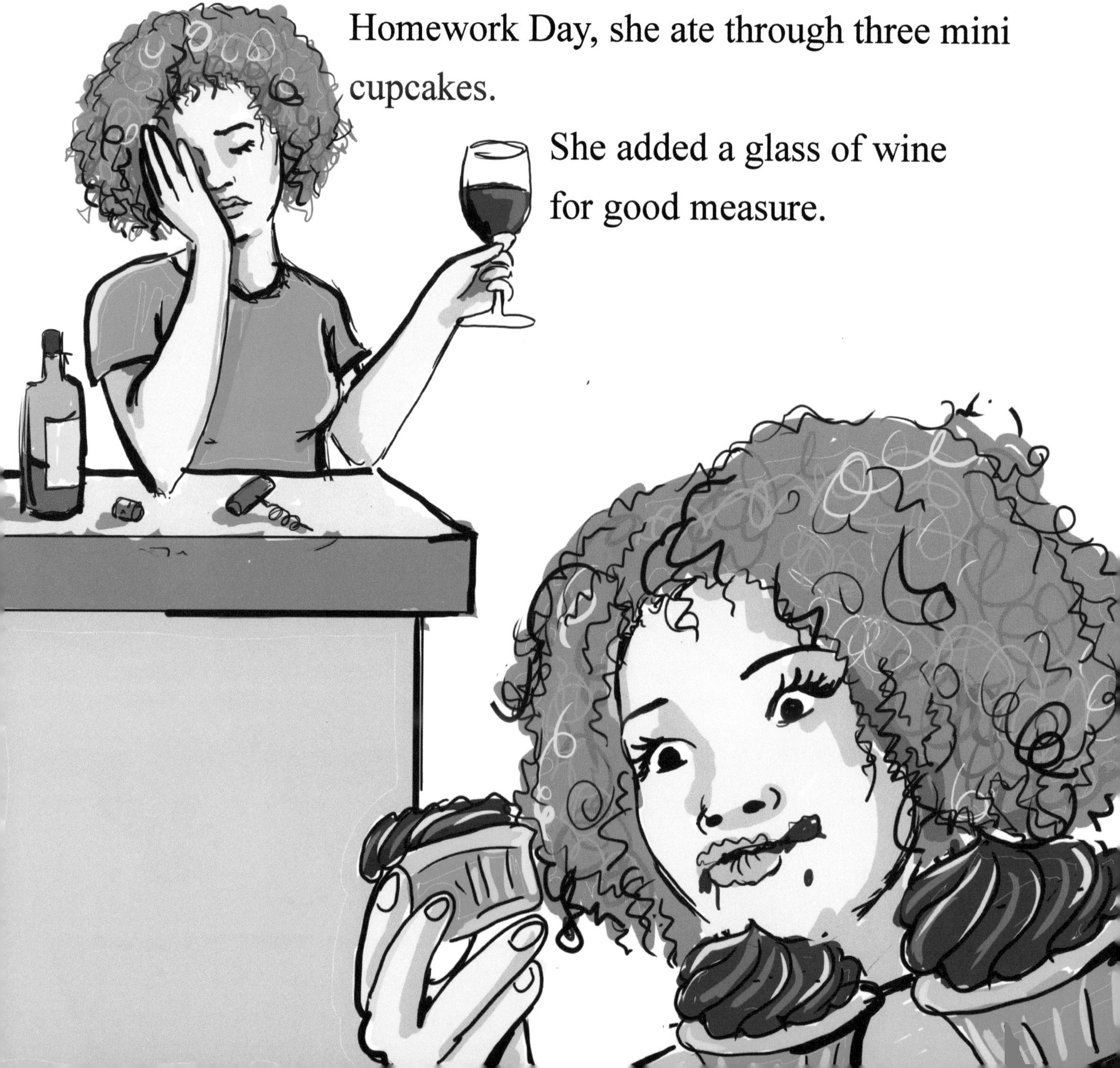

I can do this, she thought to herself.

But she was still tired and hungry.

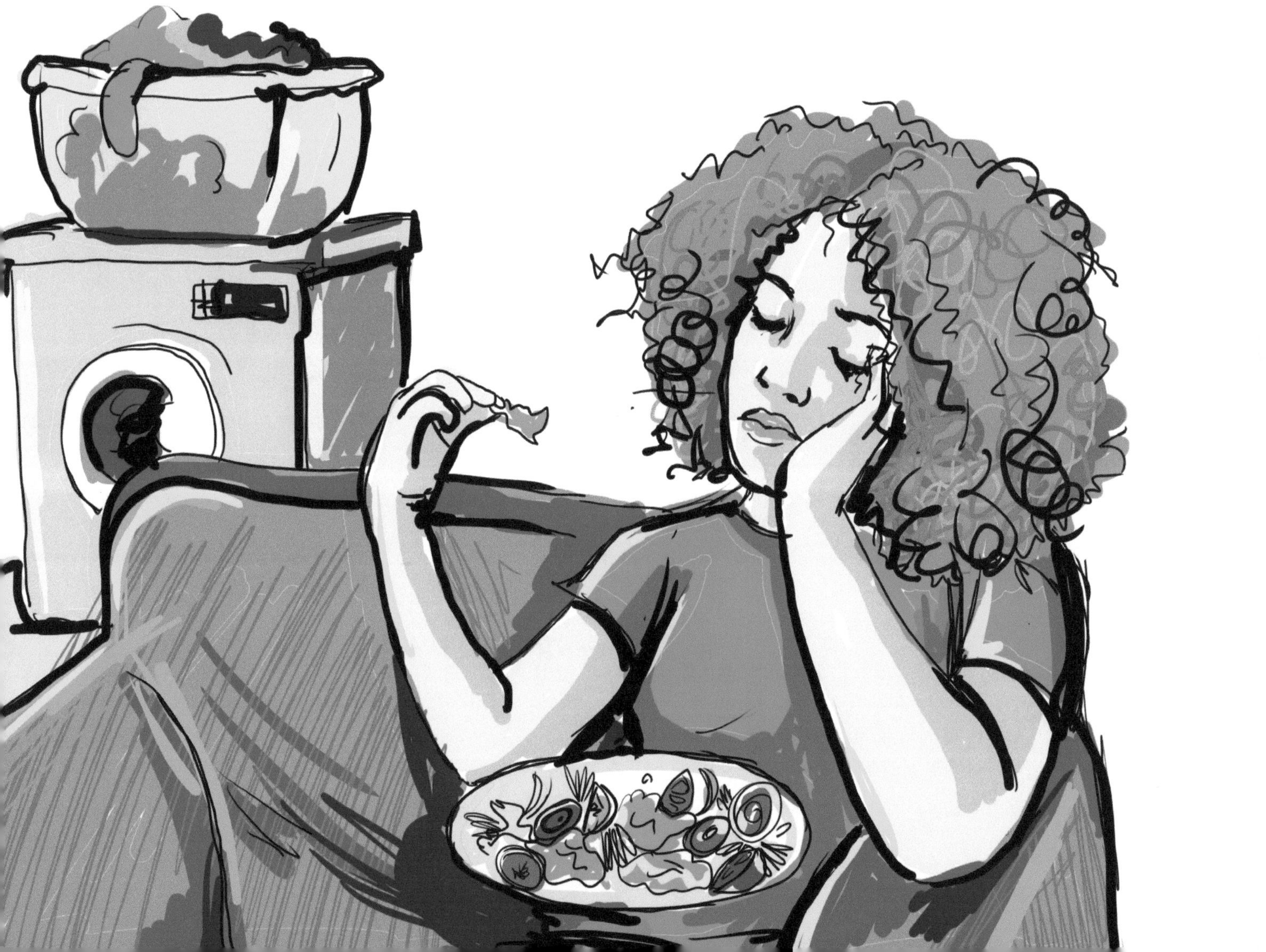

On Thursday, she ate through four tacos
when the kids asked for help with schoolwork
at the same time.

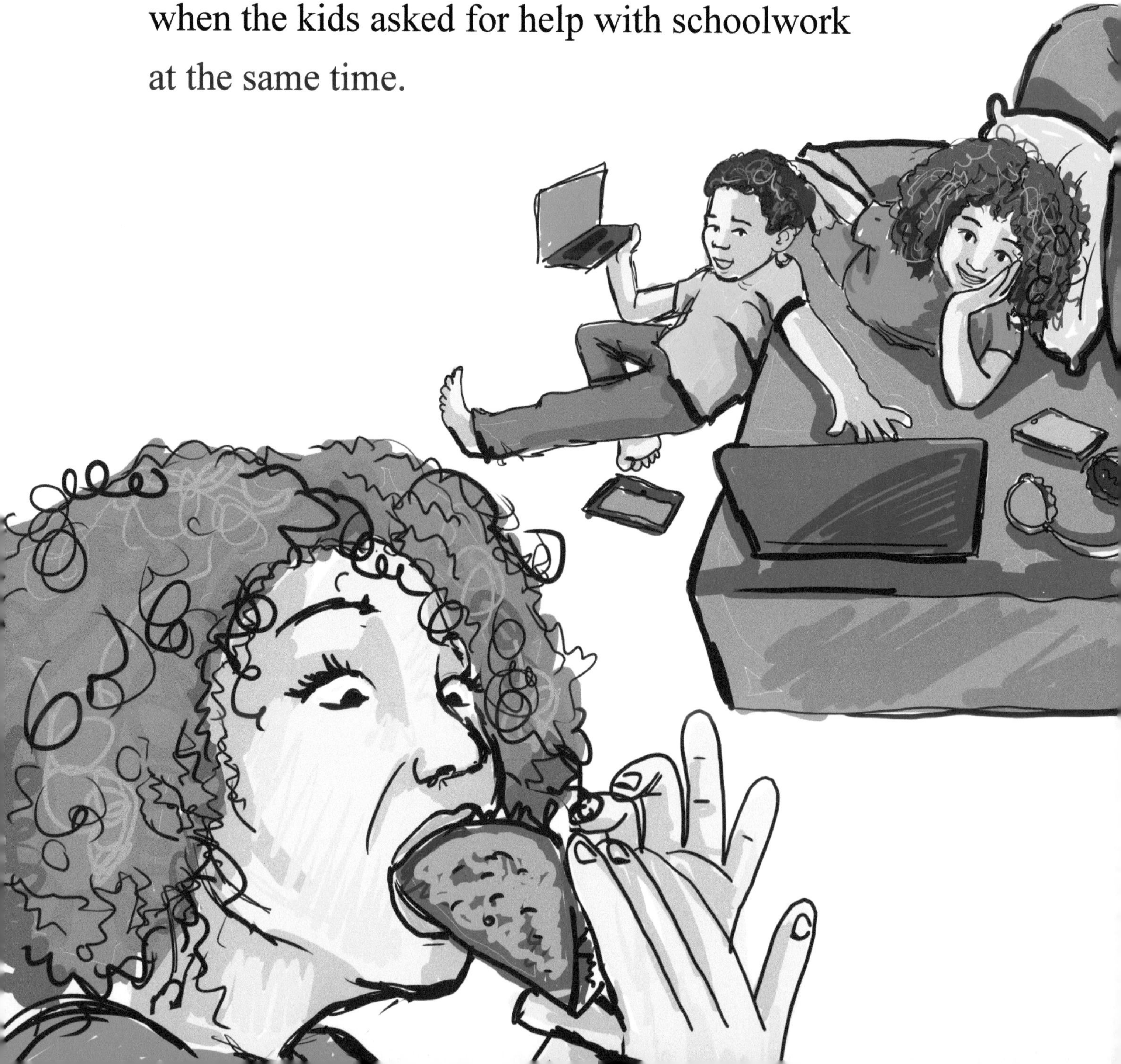

How long will this distance learning go on? she thought.

But she was still tired and hungry

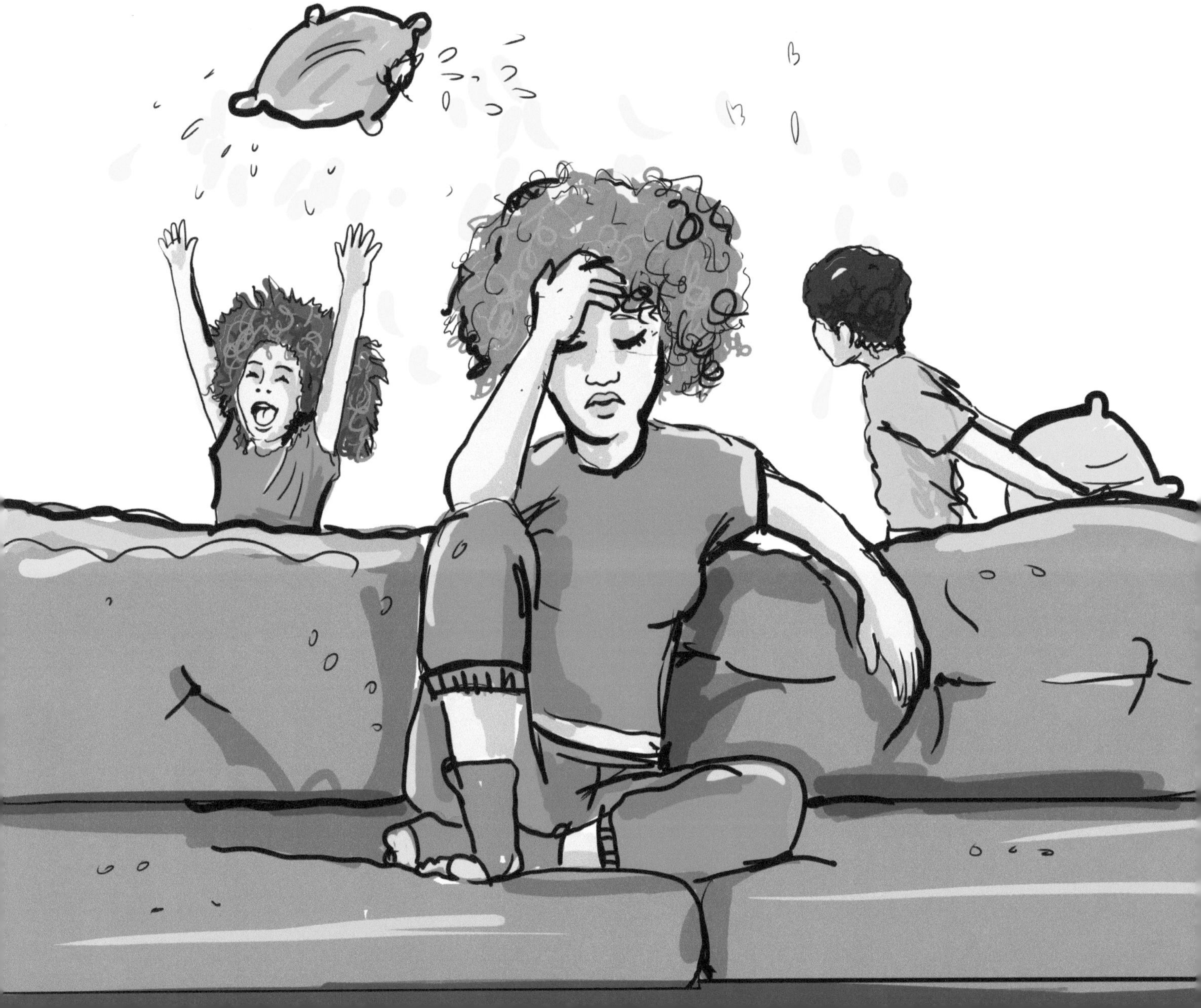

On Friday, the kids fought against doing anymore schoolwork. She sobbed in the closet and ate through five slices of pizza and a shot of tequila.

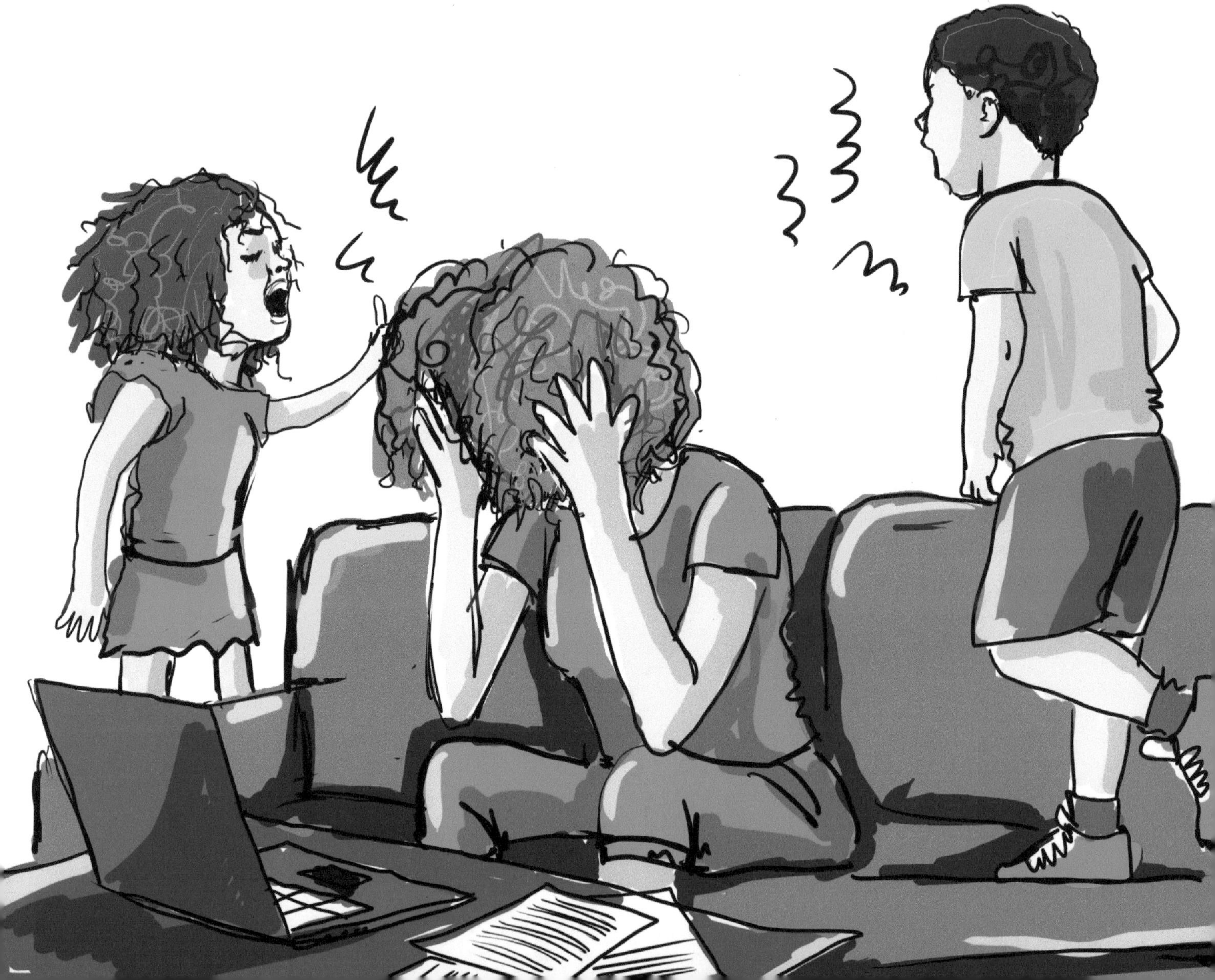

But she was still tired and hungry.

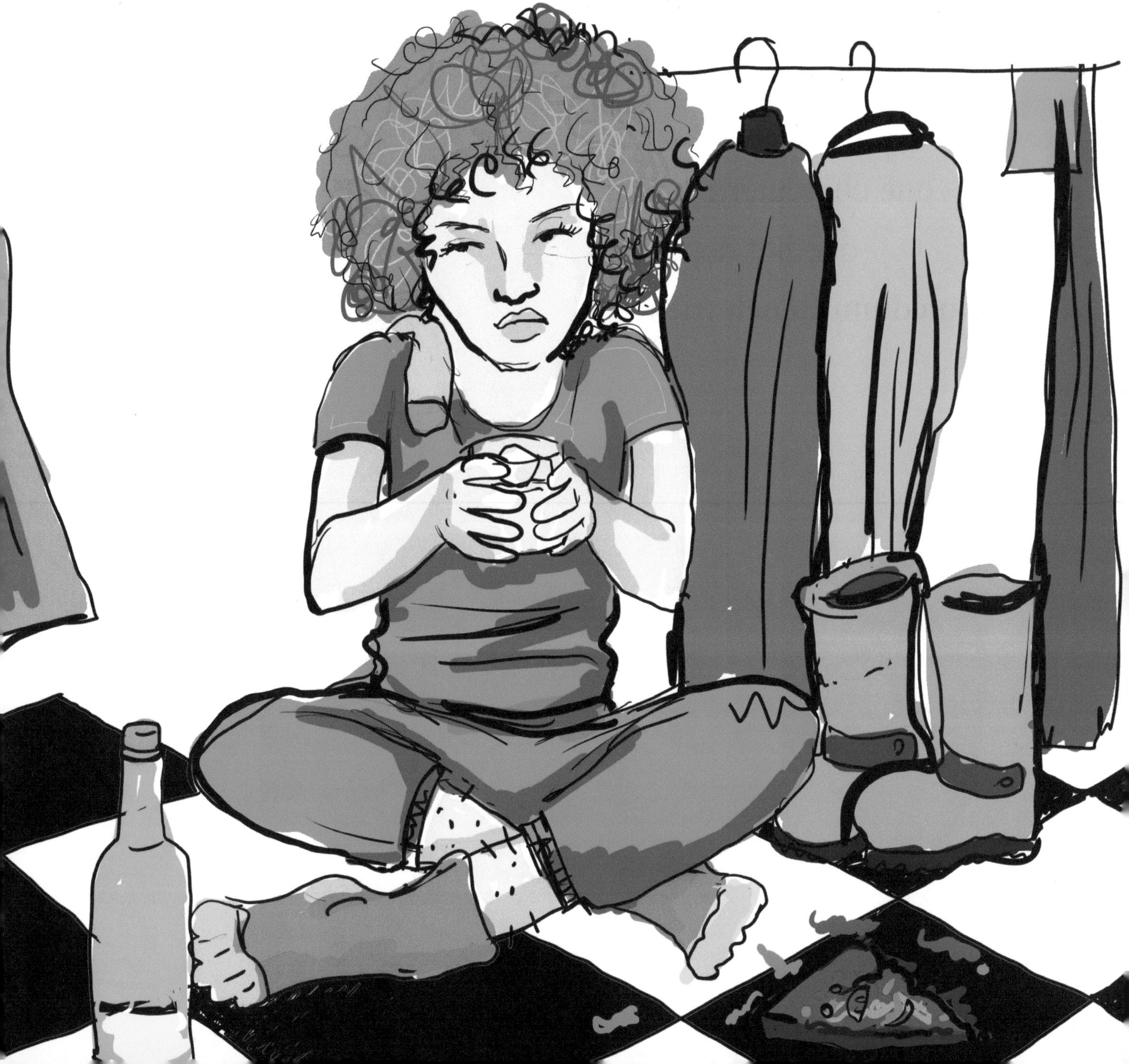

On Saturday she ate through...
one piece of chantilly cake...
one fudge popsicle...
one pickle...
one charcuterie board...
one hot dog...
one medium french fries...

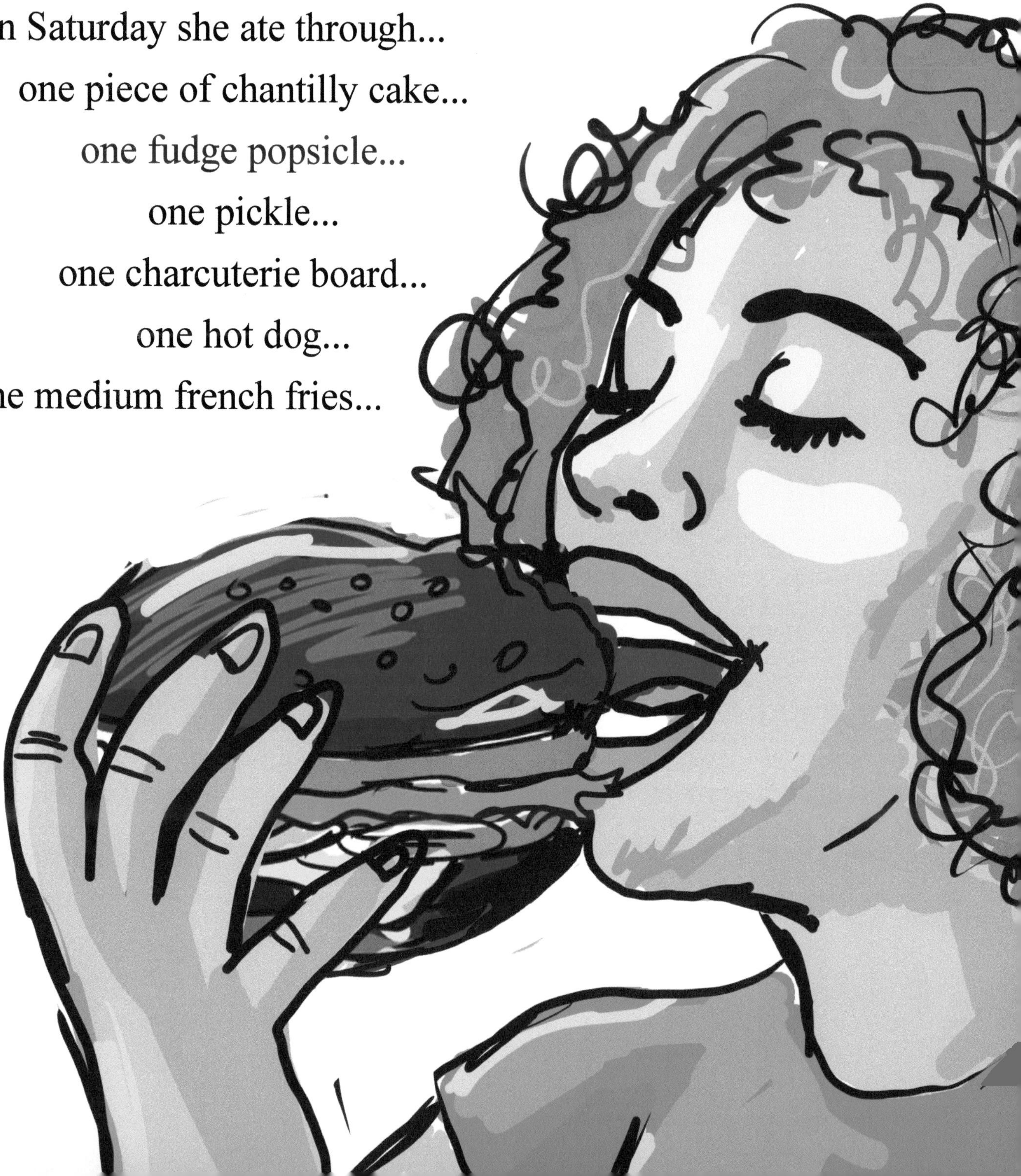

one apple pie...

one burger...

one cupcake...

and one slice of watermelon.

That night she had a

terrible stomach-ache!

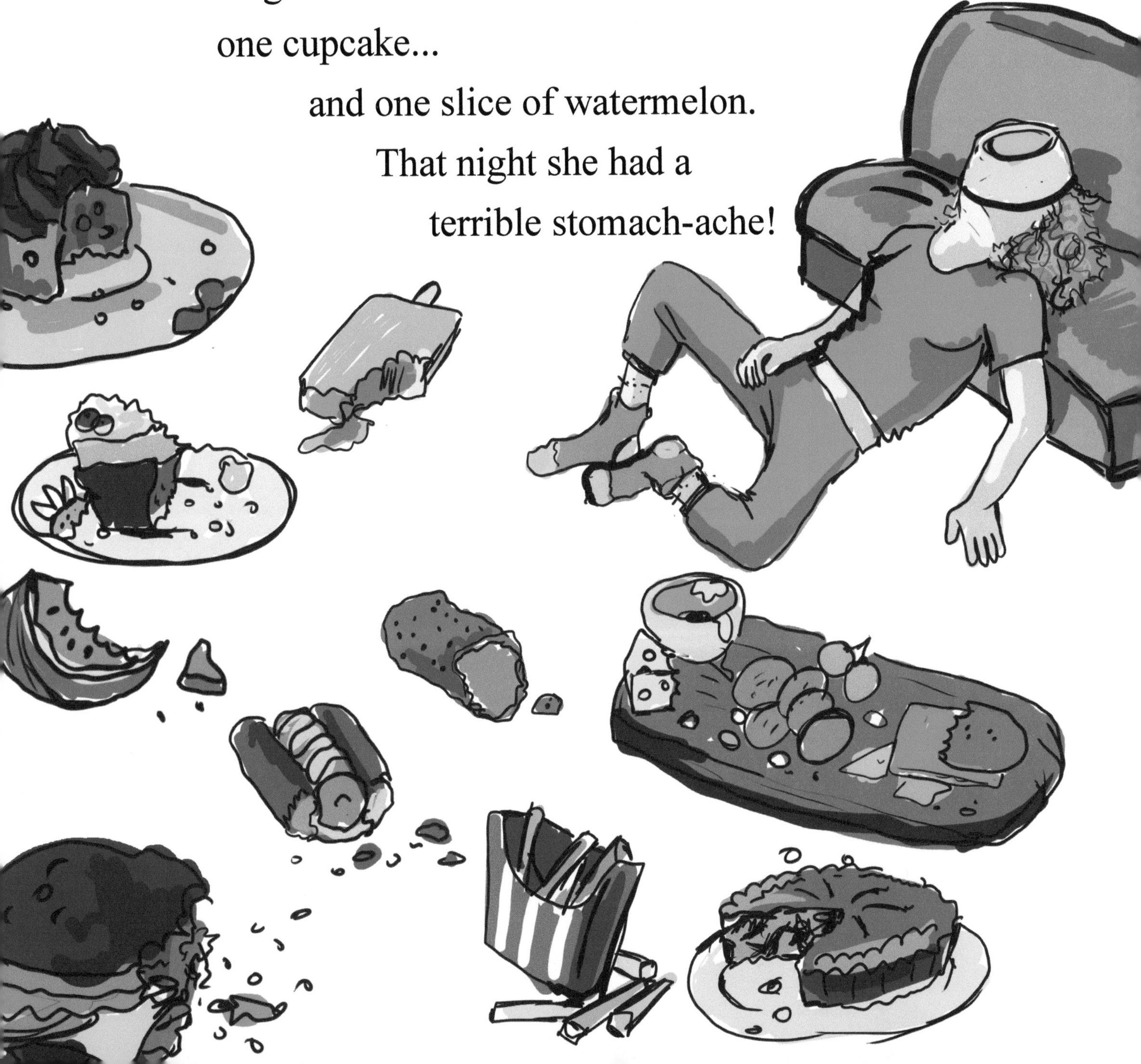

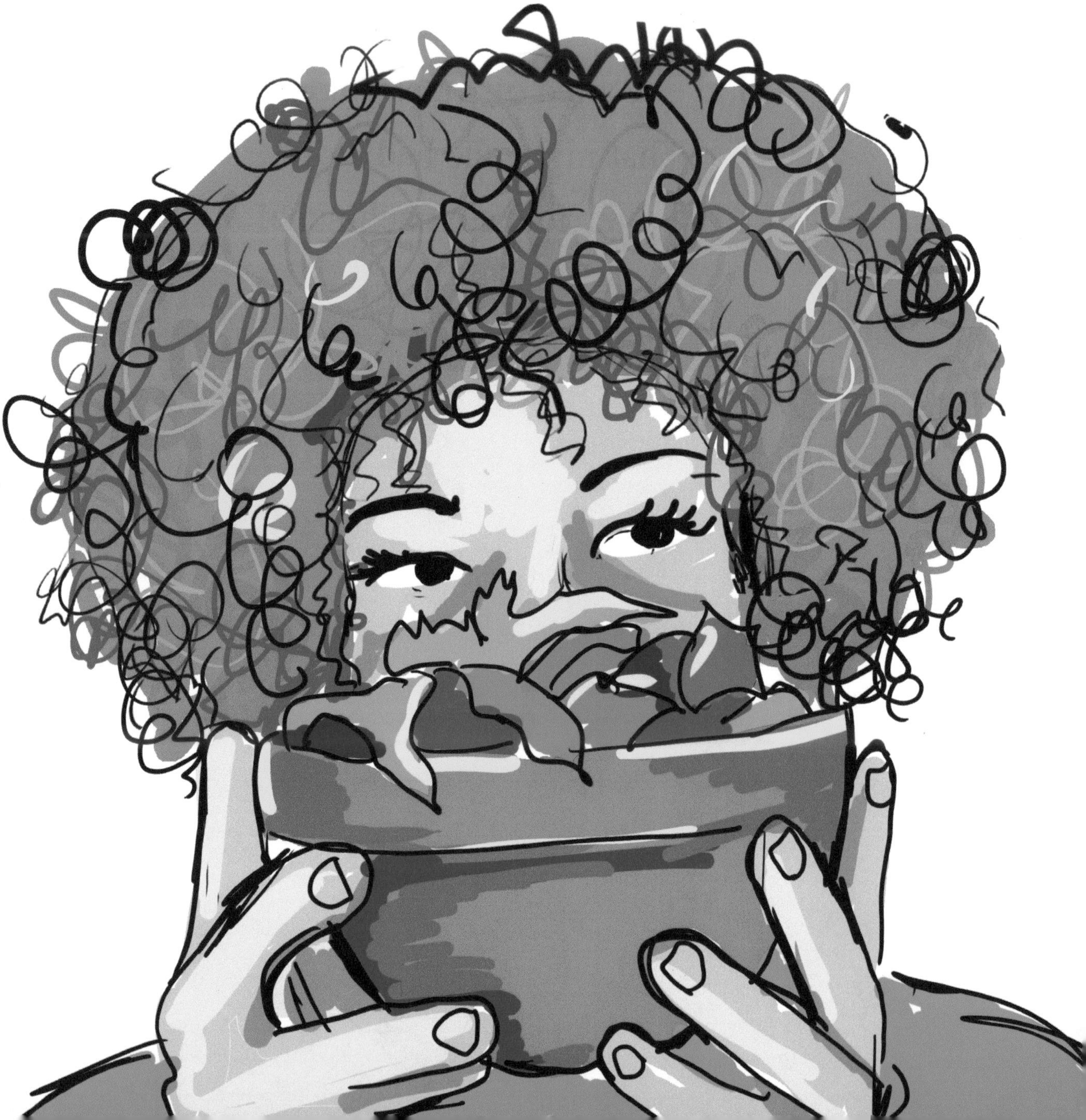

The next day was Sunday again.
She ate through one nice green salad and
announced unlimited screen time.

After that, she felt much better.

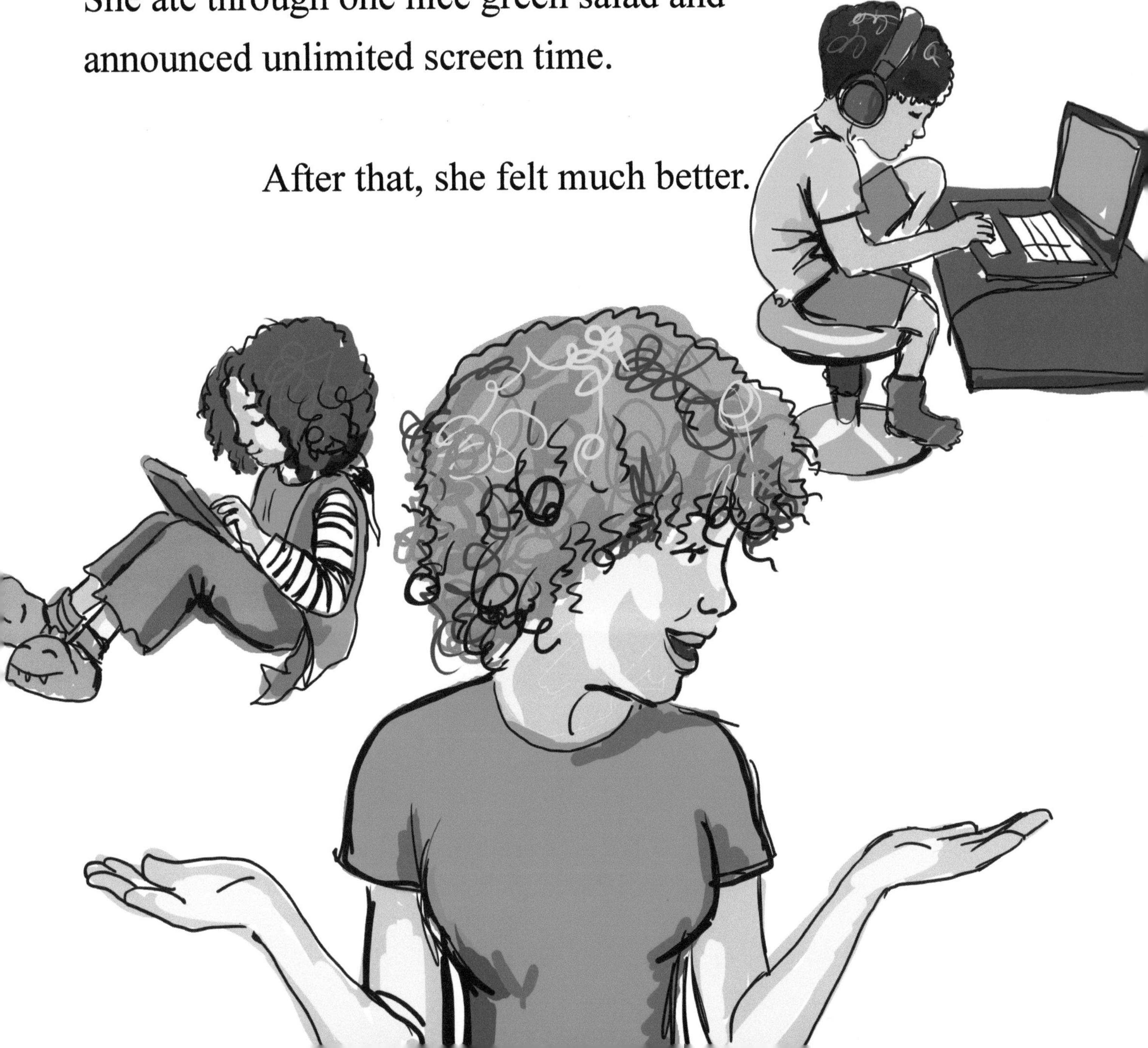

"If you need anything else, just ask daddy,"
she said as she ran into the bedroom.

She wrapped herself into a sushi roll...

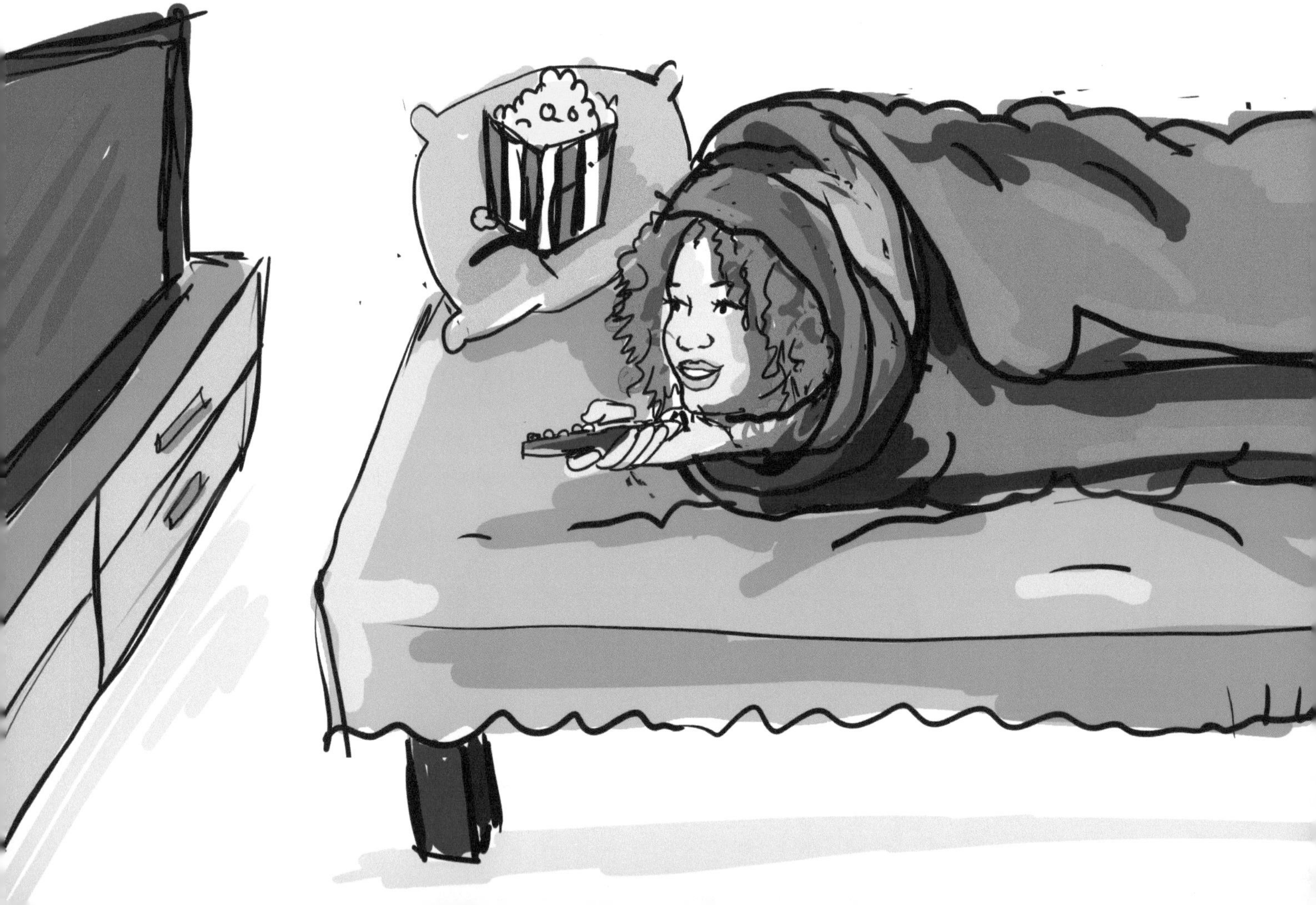

Shopped online and relaxed in a nice, hot bath.

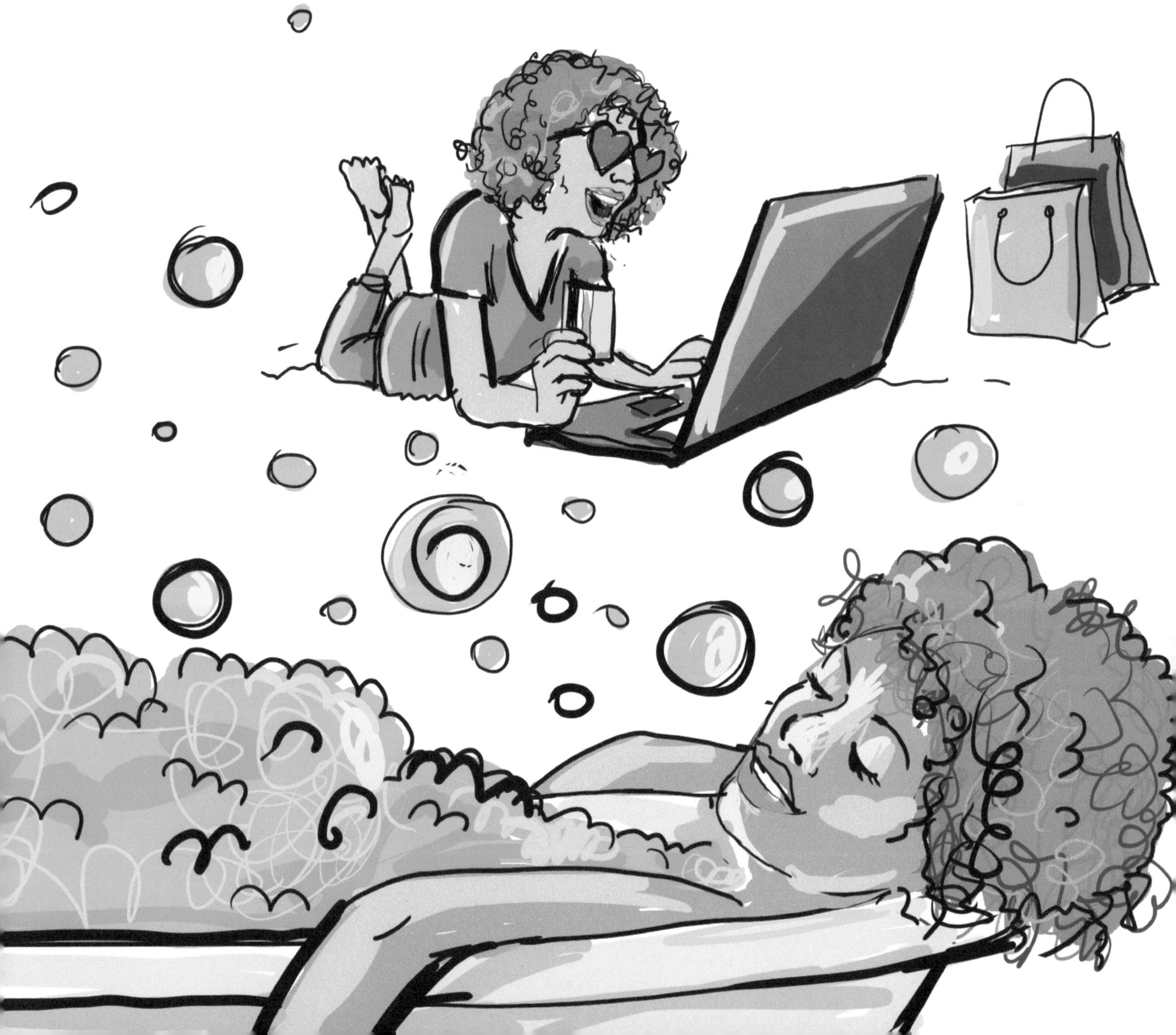

The next day, she pushed her way out and started all over again.

Mommies are amazing.

We can't pour from an empty cup so it's important to take time for self love and care, even if you have to wrap yourself into a sushi roll.

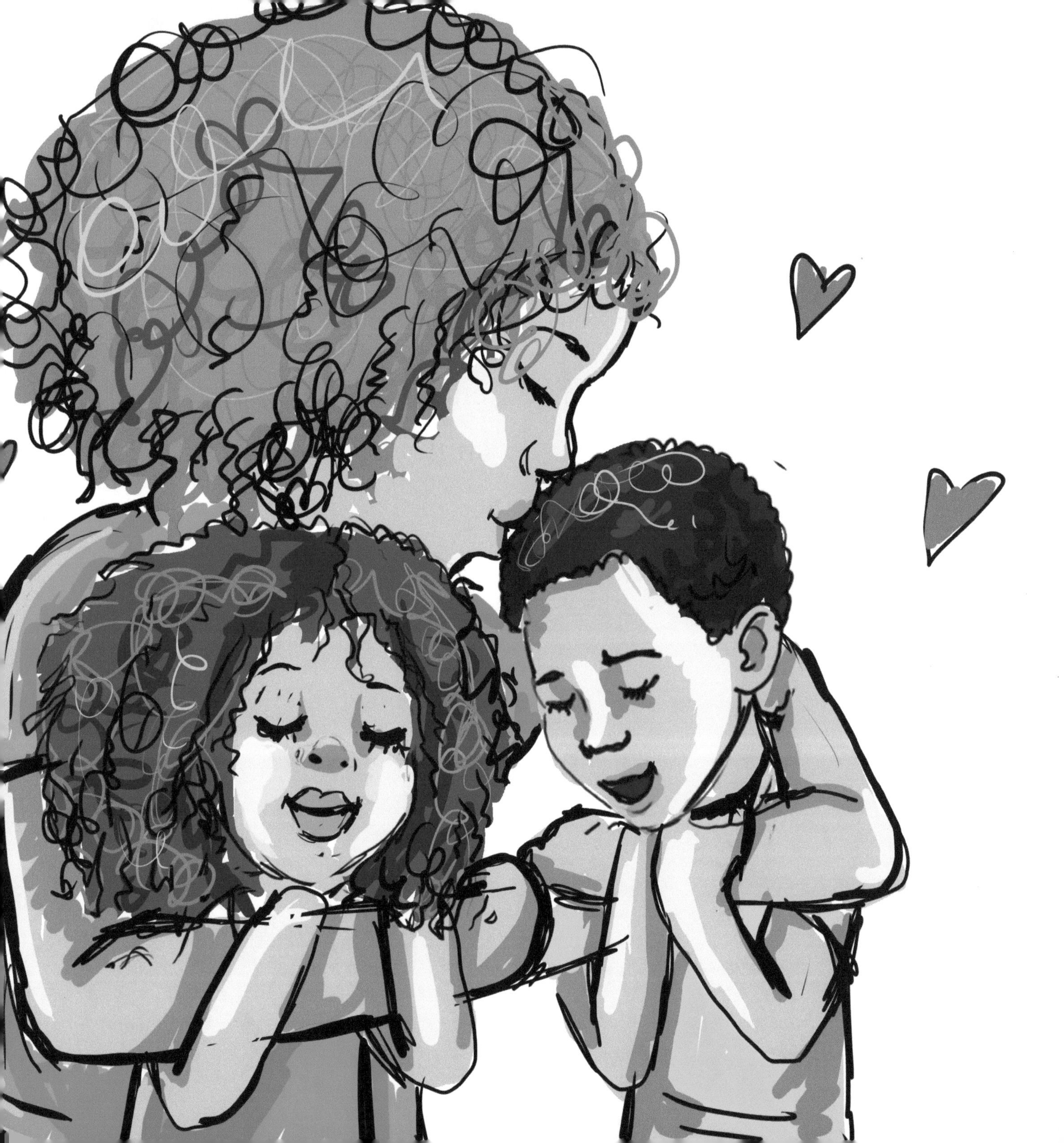

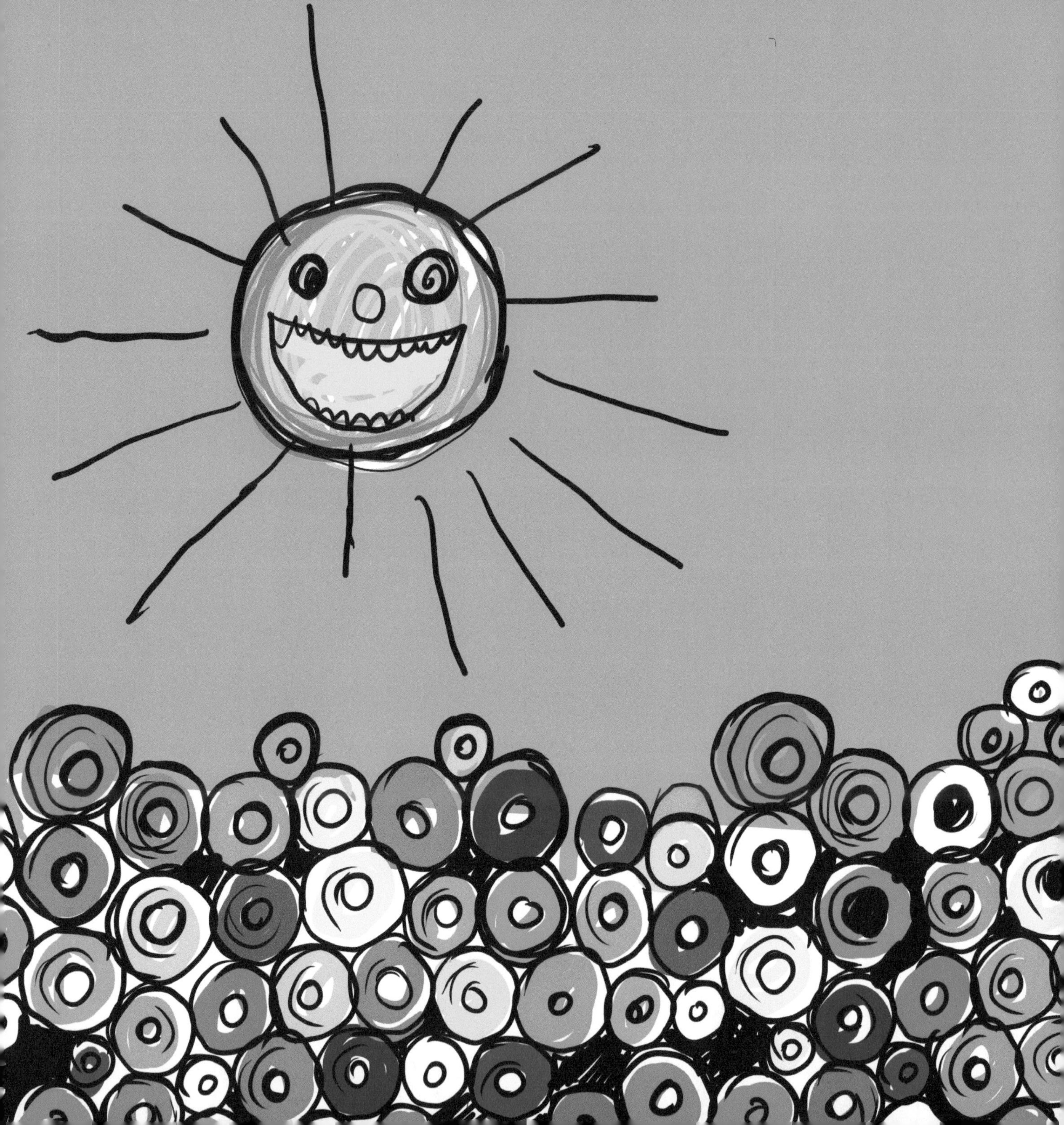

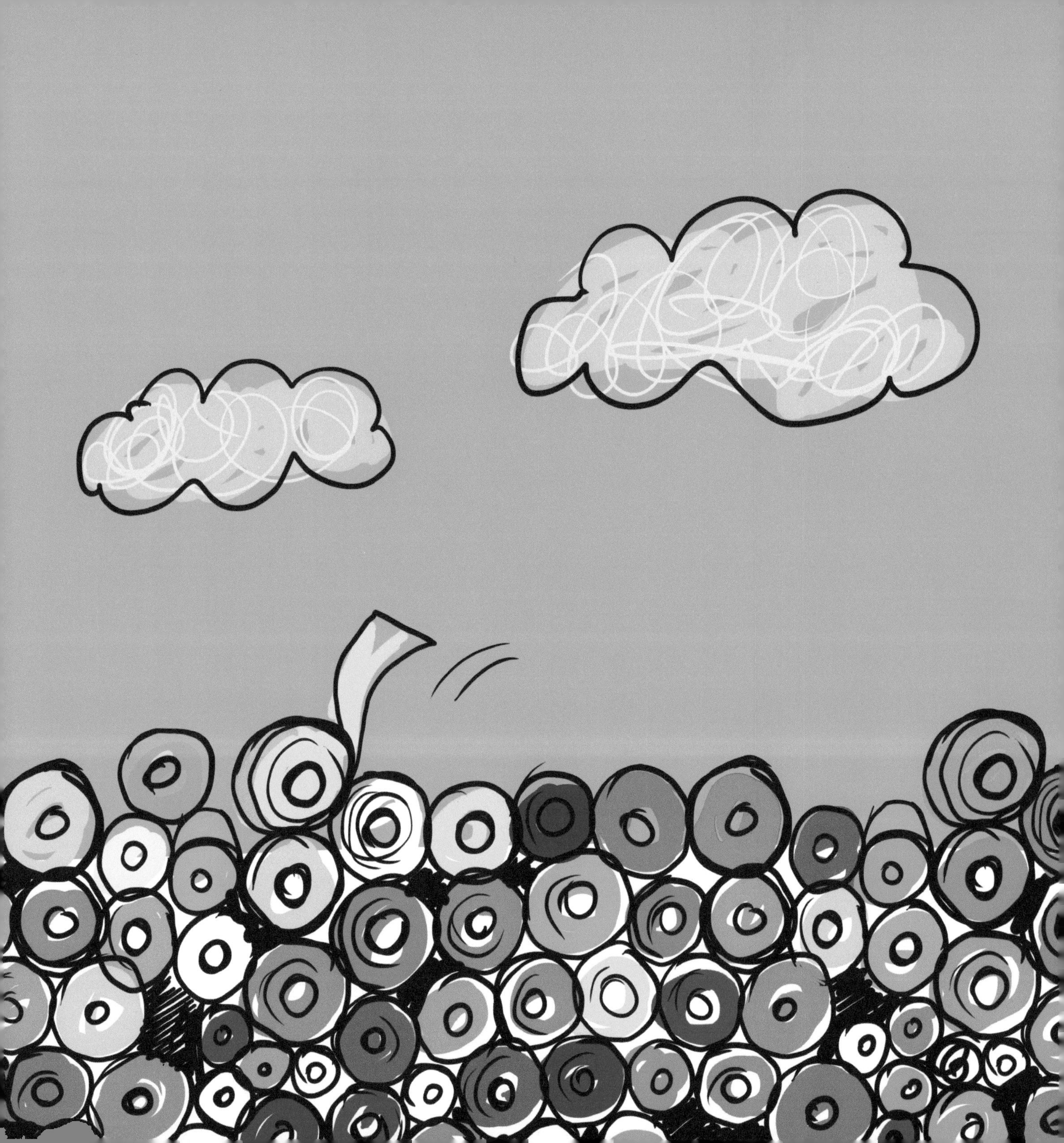

CPSIA information can be obtained
at www.ICGtesting.com
Printed in the USA
BVHW021317301020
592040BV00002B/22

* 9 7 8 1 9 5 3 3 9 9 6 5 6 *